BRITTEN & BRÜLIGHTLY

Britten & Brülightly

Hannah Berry

Jonathan Cape
London

THE FOLLOWING PEOPLE DESERVE ACKNOWLEDGEMENT

NIGEL BALDWIN, the man who encouraged me to write and rewrite and rewrite until my ears bled, for being right every time; EMILY GRAVETT, for providing a discerning eye, a sympathetic ear, and beans on toast; MUM, DAD and CHRIS, for unconditional (and often undeserved) love and support; and all those other good friends who know who they are and will forgive me for not naming them for fear of accidental omission. You are, all of you, a tribute to humanity.

This book was also assisted by a grant from THE AUTHORS' FOUNDATION, for which I am extremely grateful.

Published by Jonathan Cape 2008
Random House,
20 Vauxhall Bridge Road,
London SW1V 2SA
www.rbooks.co.uk

2 4 6 8 10 9 7 5 3

First published in Great Britain in 2008 by Jonathan Cape

Addresses for companies within The Random House Group Limited can be found at: www.randomhouse.co.uk/offices.htm

The Random House Group Limited Reg. No. 954009

A CIP catalogue record for this book is available from the British Library

ISBN 9780224077903

The Random House Group Limited makes every effort to ensure that the
papers used in our books are made from trees that have been legally
sourced from well-managed and credibly certified forests. Our paper
procurement policy can be found on www.rbooks.co.uk/environment

Printed and bound in China by C & C Offset Printing Co., Ltd

For
Nan and Granddad,
'Bita y 'Bito

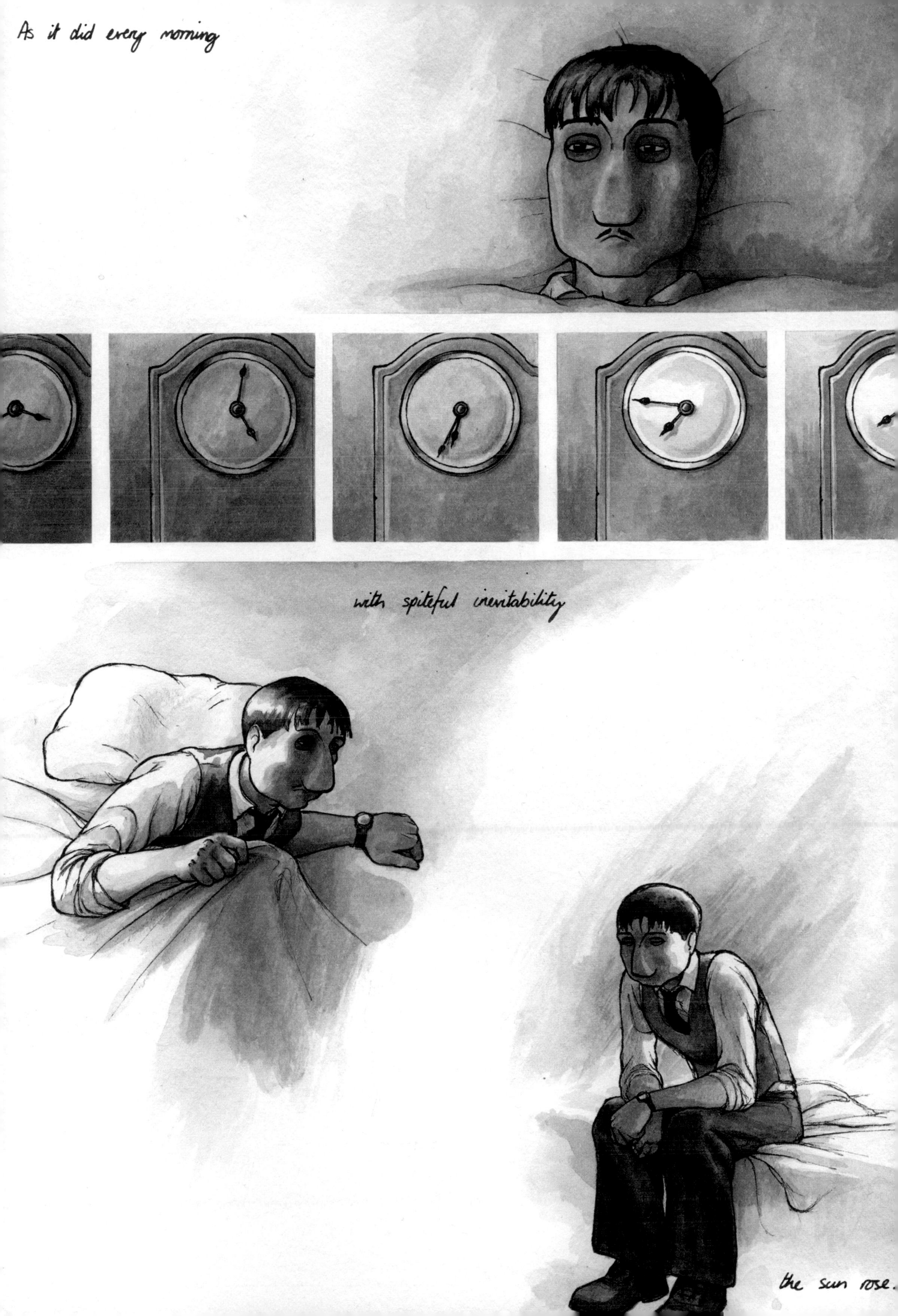
As it did every morning
with spiteful inevitability
the sun rose.

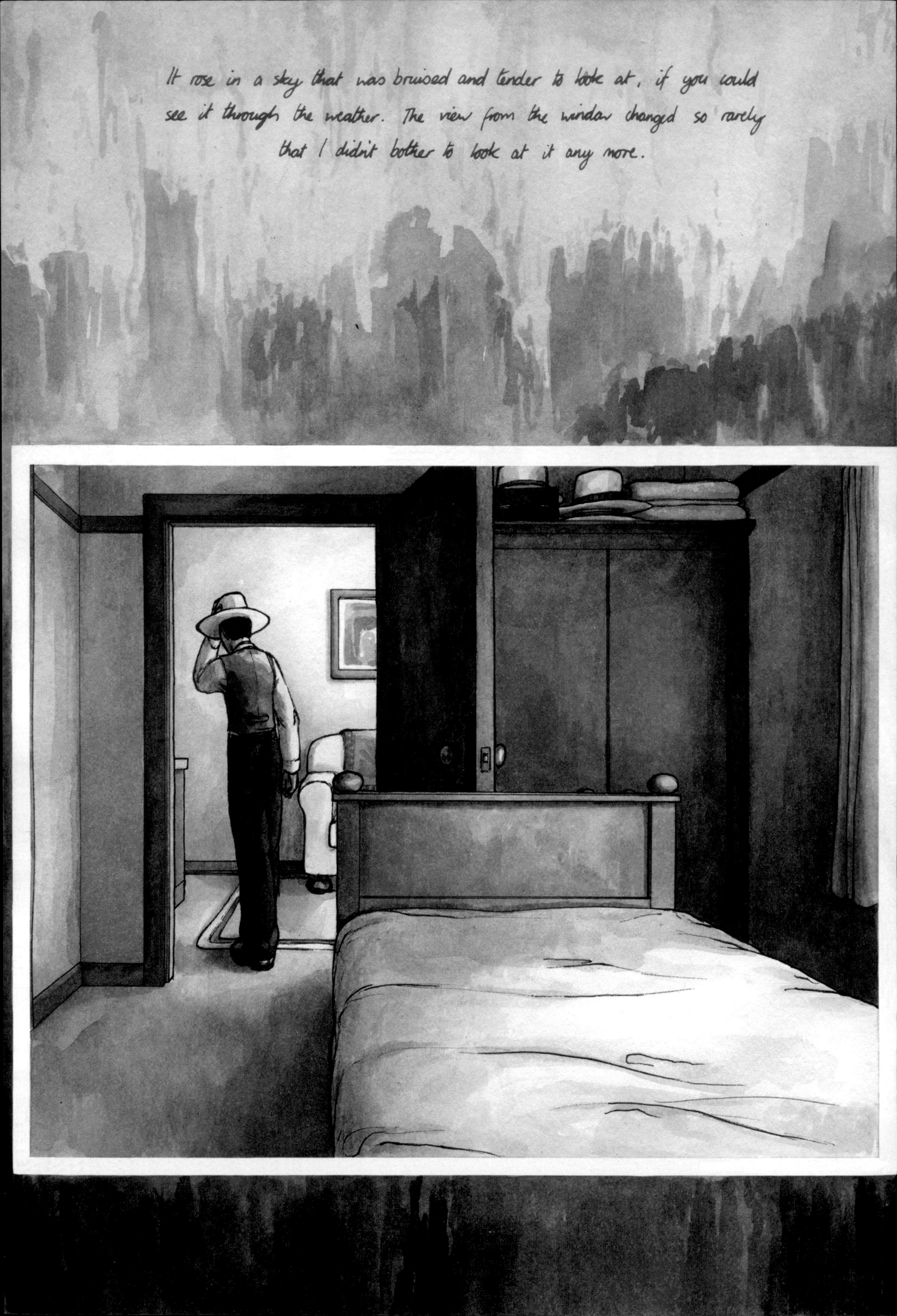
It rose in a sky that was bruised and tender to look at, if you could see it through the weather. The view from the window changed so rarely that I didn't bother to look at it any more.

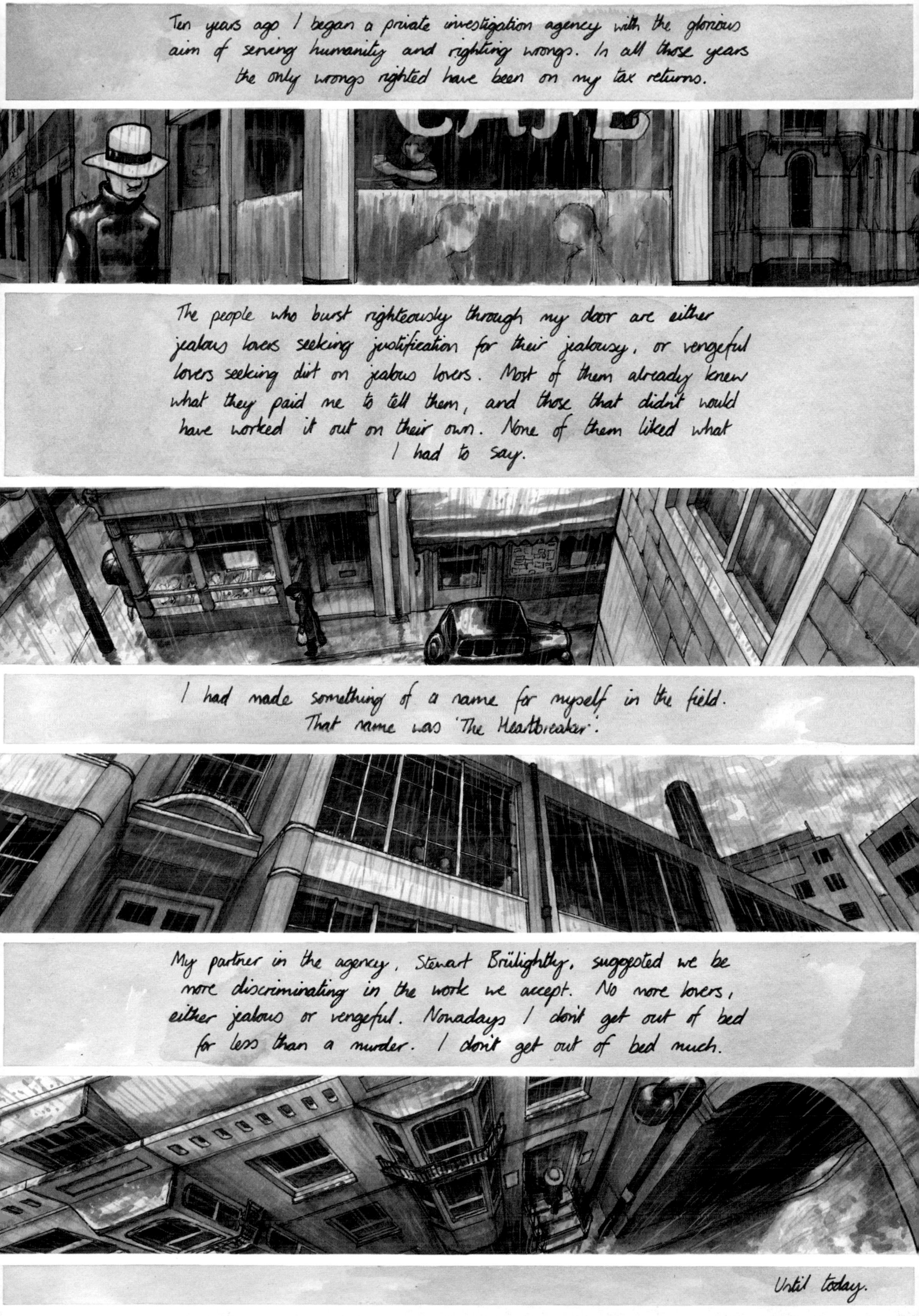
Ten years ago I began a private investigation agency with the glorious aim of serving humanity and righting wrongs. In all those years the only wrongs righted have been on my tax returns.
The people who burst righteously through my door are either jealous lovers seeking justification for their jealousy, or vengeful lovers seeking dirt on jealous lovers. Most of them already knew what they paid me to tell them, and those that didn't would have worked it out on their own. None of them liked what I had to say.
I had made something of a name for myself in the field. That name was 'The Heartbreaker'.
My partner in the agency, Stewart Brülightly, suggested we be more discriminating in the work we accept. No more lovers, either jealous or vengeful. Nowadays I don't get out of bed for less than a murder. I don't get out of bed much.
Until today.

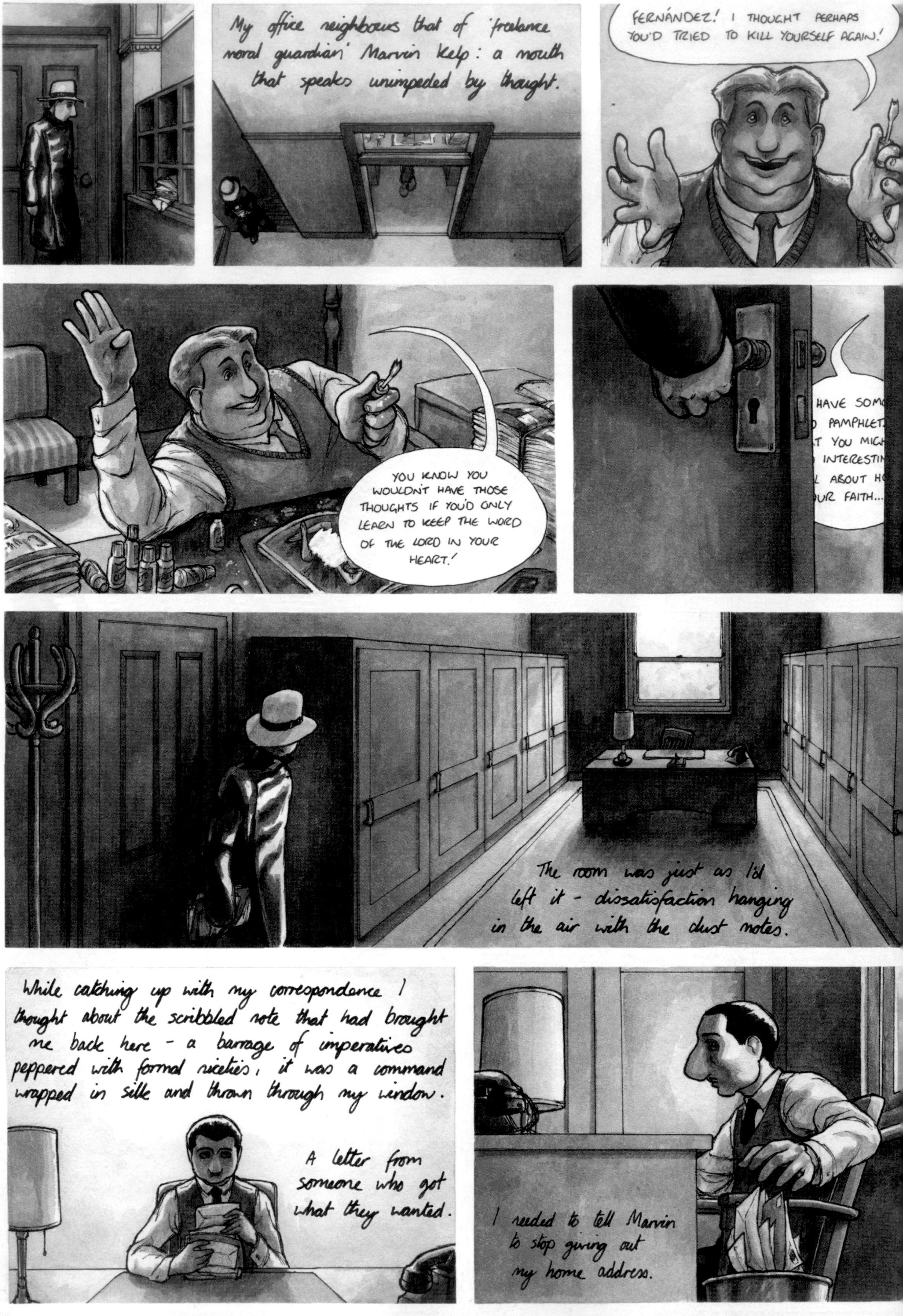

My office neighbours that of 'freelance moral guardian' Marvin Kelp: a mouth that speaks unimpeded by thought.
FERNÁNDEZ! I THOUGHT PERHAPS YOU'D TRIED TO KILL YOURSELF AGAIN!
YOU KNOW YOU WOULDN'T HAVE THOSE THOUGHTS IF YOU'D ONLY LEARN TO KEEP THE WORD OF THE LORD IN YOUR HEART!
HAVE SOM PAMPHLET T YOU MIGH INTERESTIN L ABOUT HO UR FAITH...
The room was just as I'd left it - dissatisfaction hanging in the air with the dust motes.
While catching up with my correspondence I thought about the scribbled note that had brought me back here - a barrage of imperatives peppered with formal niceties, it was a command wrapped in silk and thrown through my window.
A letter from someone who got what they wanted.
I needed to tell Marvin to stop giving out my home address.

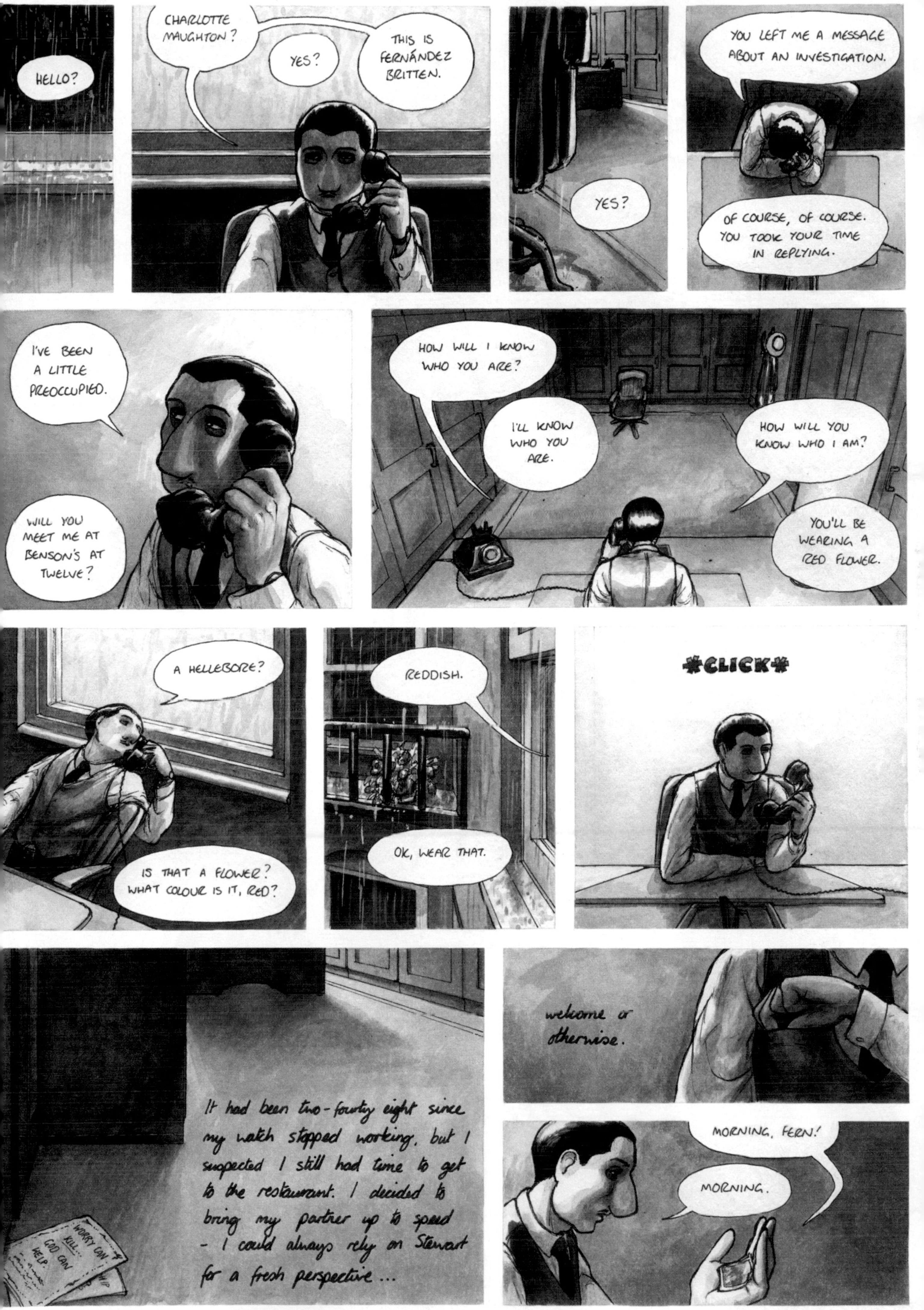

HELLO?
CHARLOTTE MAUGHTON?
YES?
THIS IS FERNÁNDEZ BRITTEN.
YES?
YOU LEFT ME A MESSAGE ABOUT AN INVESTIGATION.
OF COURSE, OF COURSE. YOU TOOK YOUR TIME IN REPLYING.
I'VE BEEN A LITTLE PREOCCUPIED.
WILL YOU MEET ME AT BENSON'S AT TWELVE?
HOW WILL I KNOW WHO YOU ARE?
I'LL KNOW WHO YOU ARE.
HOW WILL YOU KNOW WHO I AM?
YOU'LL BE WEARING A RED FLOWER.
A HELLEBORE?
IS THAT A FLOWER? WHAT COLOUR IS IT, RED?
REDDISH.
OK, WEAR THAT.
CLICK
It had been two-fourty eight since my watch stopped working, but I suspected I still had time to get to the restaurant. I decided to bring my partner up to speed - I could always rely on Stewart for a fresh perspective ...
WORRY CAN KILL. GOD CAN HELP.
welcome or otherwise.
MORNING, FERN!
MORNING.

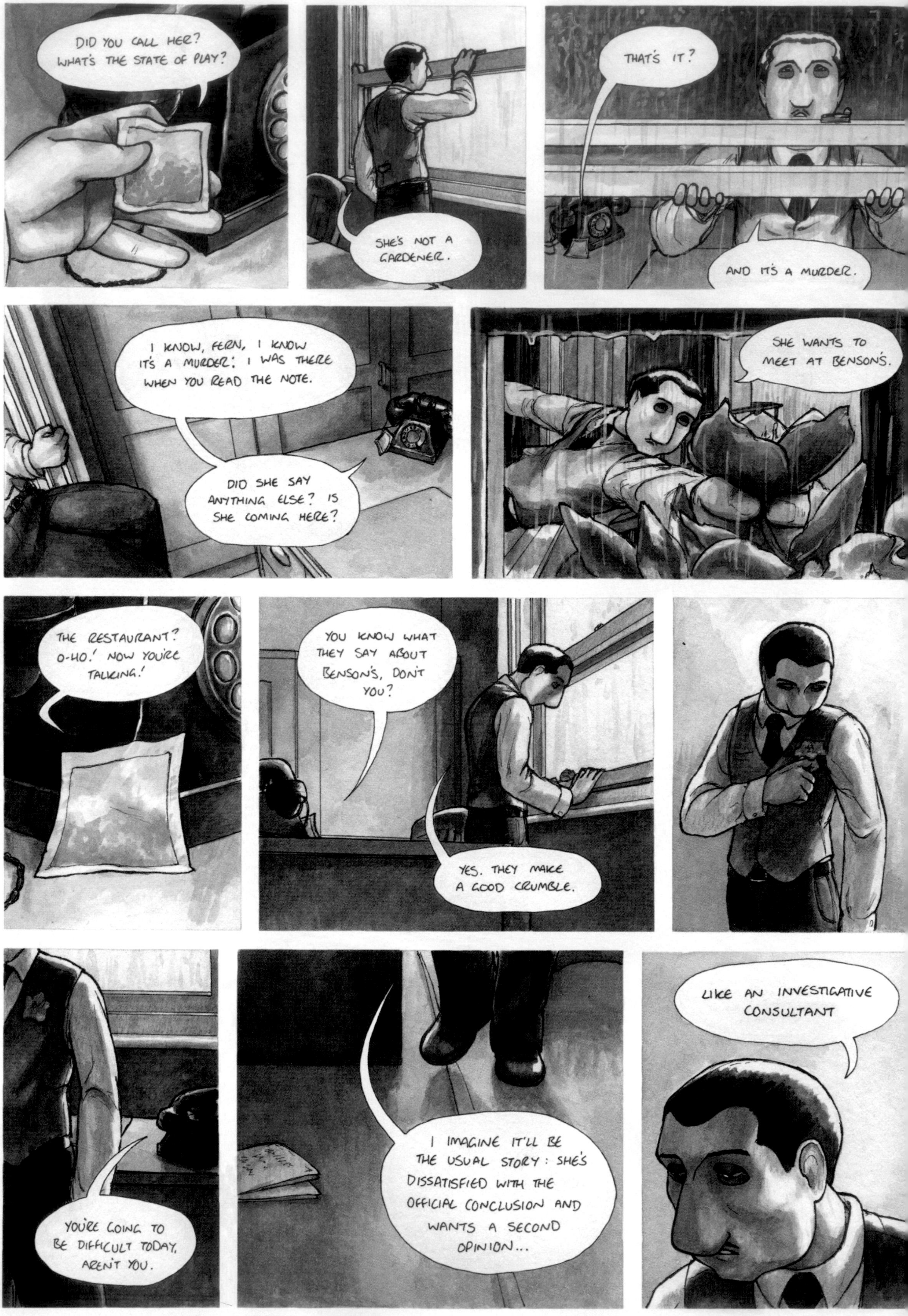
DID YOU CALL HER? WHAT'S THE STATE OF PLAY?
SHE'S NOT A GARDENER.
THAT'S IT?
AND IT'S A MURDER.
I KNOW, FERN, I KNOW IT'S A MURDER: I WAS THERE WHEN YOU READ THE NOTE.
DID SHE SAY ANYTHING ELSE? IS SHE COMING HERE?
SHE WANTS TO MEET AT BENSON'S.
THE RESTAURANT? O-HO! NOW YOU'RE TALKING!
YOU KNOW WHAT THEY SAY ABOUT BENSON'S, DON'T YOU?
YES. THEY MAKE A GOOD CRUMBLE.
YOU'RE GOING TO BE DIFFICULT TODAY, AREN'T YOU.
I IMAGINE IT'LL BE THE USUAL STORY: SHE'S DISSATISFIED WITH THE OFFICIAL CONCLUSION AND WANTS A SECOND OPINION...
LIKE AN INVESTIGATIVE CONSULTANT

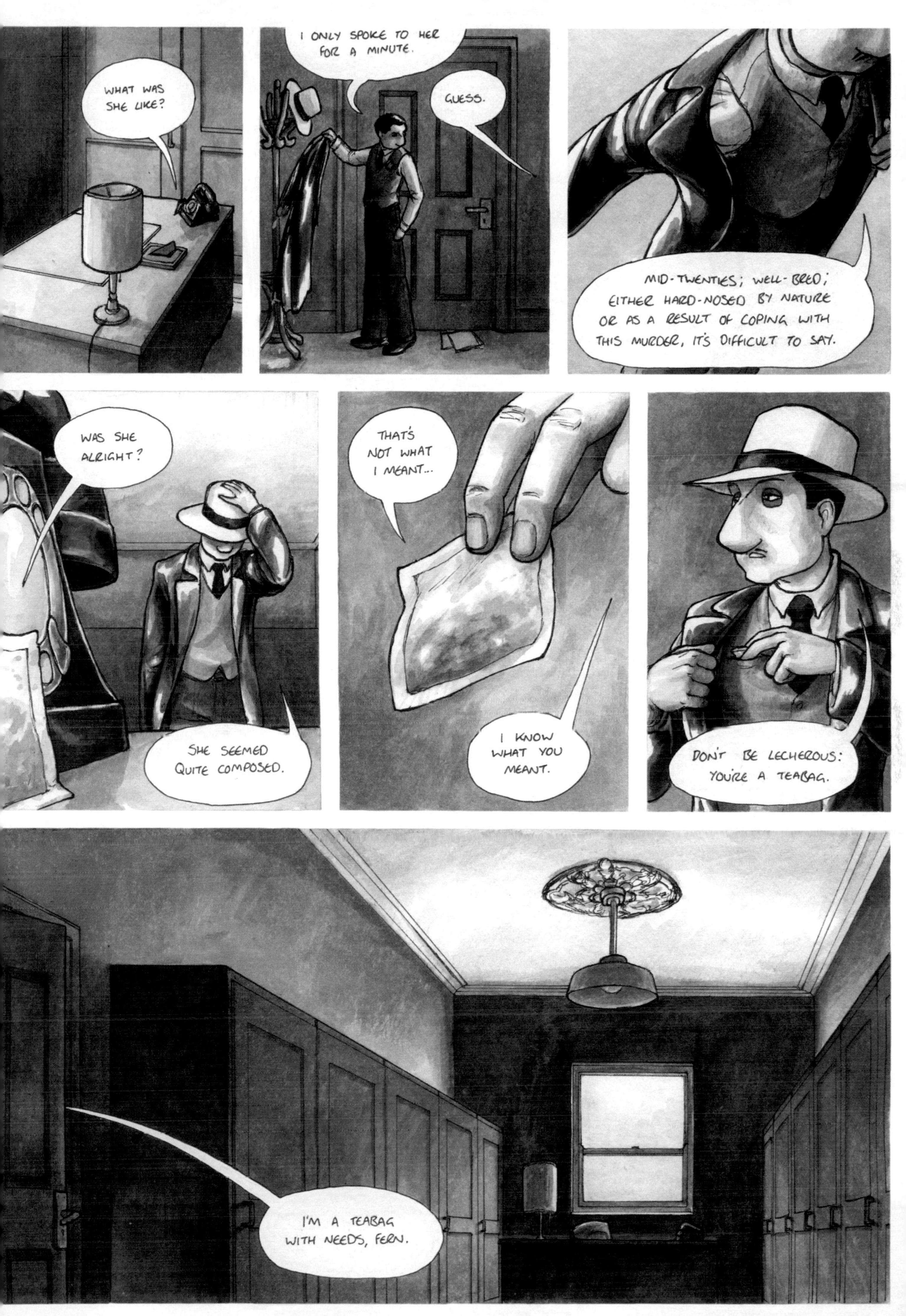
WHAT WAS SHE LIKE?
I ONLY SPOKE TO HER FOR A MINUTE.
GUESS.
MID-TWENTIES; WELL-BRED; EITHER HARD-NOSED BY NATURE OR AS A RESULT OF COPING WITH THIS MURDER, IT'S DIFFICULT TO SAY.
WAS SHE ALRIGHT?
SHE SEEMED QUITE COMPOSED.
THAT'S NOT WHAT I MEANT...
I KNOW WHAT YOU MEANT.
DON'T BE LECHEROUS: YOU'RE A TEABAG.
I'M A TEABAG WITH NEEDS, FERN.

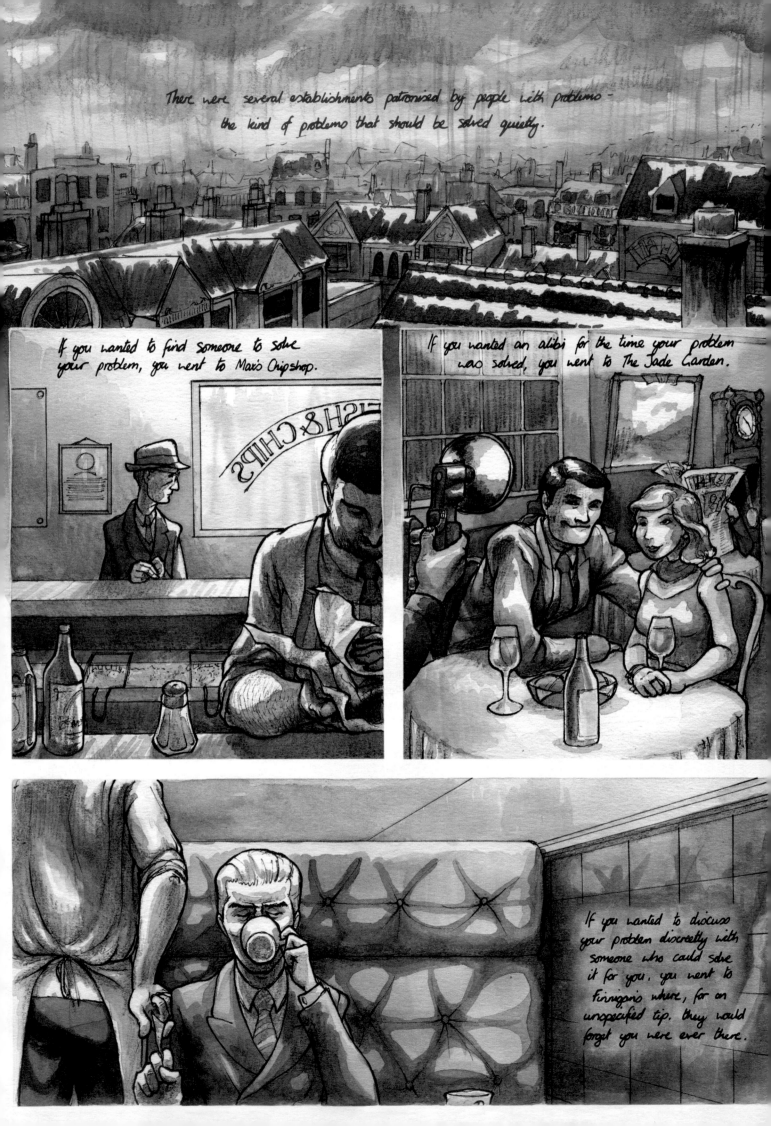

There were several establishments patronised by people with problems — the kind of problems that should be solved quietly.

If you wanted to find someone to solve your problem, you went to Max's Chipshop.

If you wanted an alibi for the time your problem was solved, you went to The Jade Garden.

If you wanted to discuss your problem discreetly with someone who could solve it for you, you went to Finnigan's where, for an unspecified tip, they would forget you were ever there.

Benson's, unknown to most, worked on a similar principle to Finnigan's: the size of the tip directly related to the sensitivity of the information the waiter was to forget they overheard.

The woman I took to be Charlotte Maughton, however, appeared blissfully unaware of this.

Gliding serenely past the troubled clientele, she looked how I imagine a swan might if it were on lithium.

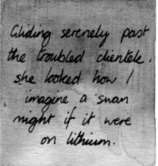

FUCKING WEATHER.

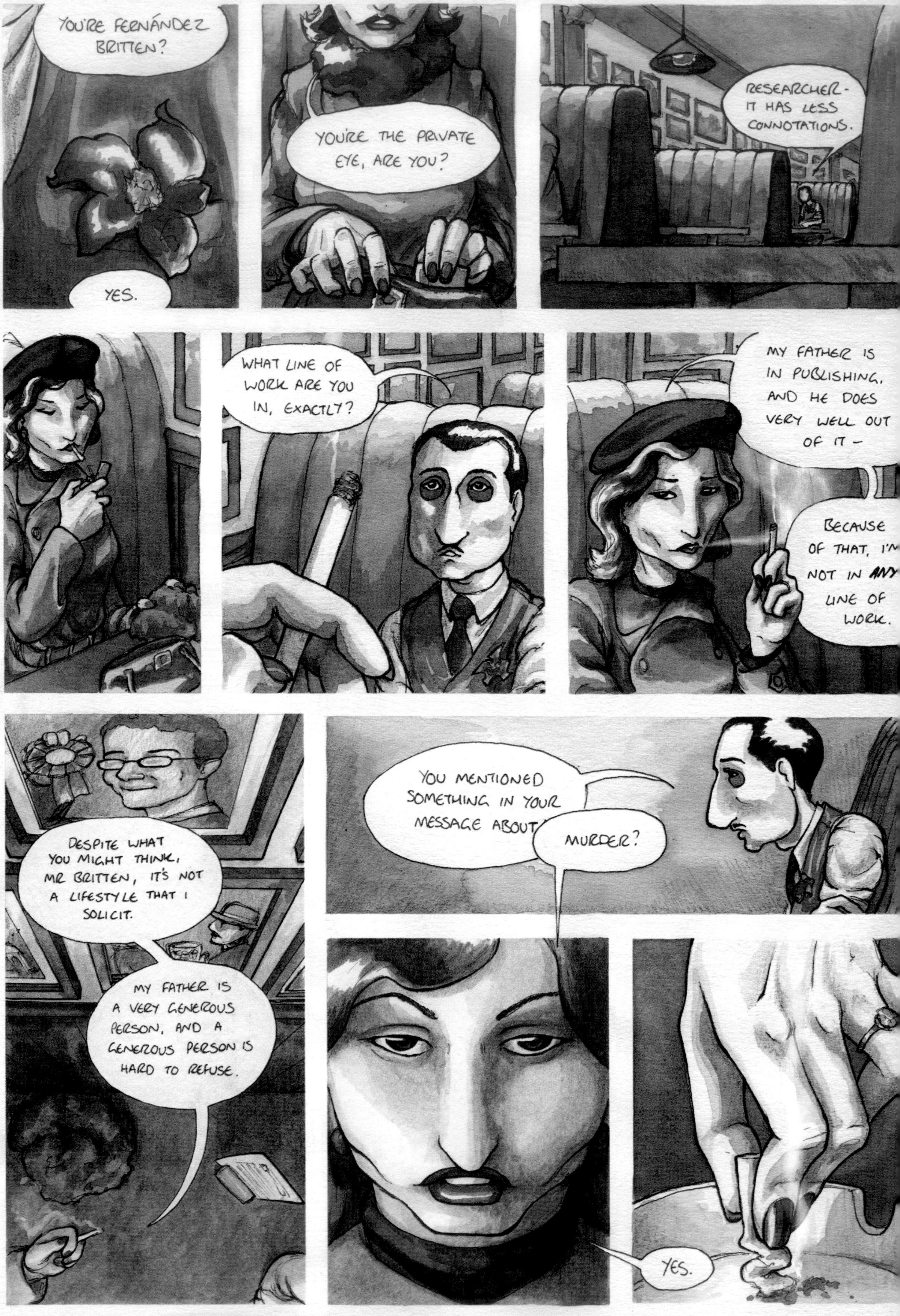
YOU'RE FERNÁNDEZ BRITTEN?
YES.
YOU'RE THE PRIVATE EYE, ARE YOU?
RESEARCHER - IT HAS LESS CONNOTATIONS.
WHAT LINE OF WORK ARE YOU IN, EXACTLY?
MY FATHER IS IN PUBLISHING, AND HE DOES VERY WELL OUT OF IT -
BECAUSE OF THAT, I'M NOT IN **ANY** LINE OF WORK.
DESPITE WHAT YOU MIGHT THINK, MR BRITTEN, IT'S NOT A LIFESTYLE THAT I SOLICIT.
MY FATHER IS A VERY GENEROUS PERSON, AND A GENEROUS PERSON IS HARD TO REFUSE.
YOU MENTIONED SOMETHING IN YOUR MESSAGE ABOUT...
MURDER?
YES.

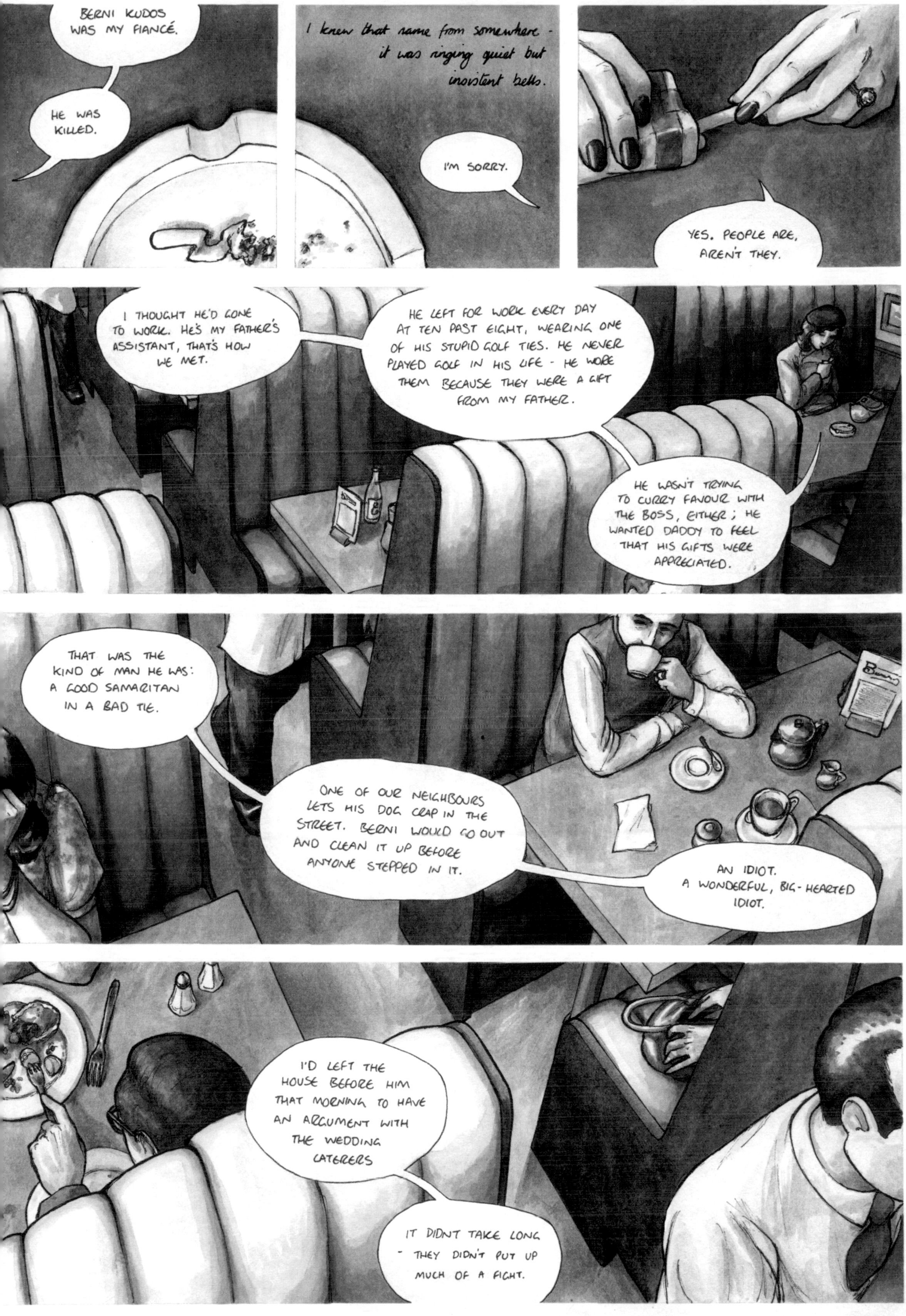
BERNI KUDOS WAS MY FIANCÉ.
HE WAS KILLED.
I knew that name from somewhere - it was ringing quiet but insistent bells.
I'M SORRY.
YES. PEOPLE ARE, AREN'T THEY.
I THOUGHT HE'D GONE TO WORK. HE'S MY FATHER'S ASSISTANT, THAT'S HOW WE MET.
HE LEFT FOR WORK EVERY DAY AT TEN PAST EIGHT, WEARING ONE OF HIS STUPID GOLF TIES. HE NEVER PLAYED GOLF IN HIS LIFE - HE WORE THEM BECAUSE THEY WERE A GIFT FROM MY FATHER.
HE WASN'T TRYING TO CURRY FAVOUR WITH THE BOSS, EITHER; HE WANTED DADDY TO FEEL THAT HIS GIFTS WERE APPRECIATED.
THAT WAS THE KIND OF MAN HE WAS: A GOOD SAMARITAN IN A BAD TIE.
ONE OF OUR NEIGHBOURS LETS HIS DOG CRAP IN THE STREET. BERNI WOULD GO OUT AND CLEAN IT UP BEFORE ANYONE STEPPED IN IT.
AN IDIOT. A WONDERFUL, BIG-HEARTED IDIOT.
I'D LEFT THE HOUSE BEFORE HIM THAT MORNING TO HAVE AN ARGUMENT WITH THE WEDDING CATERERS
IT DIDNT TAKE LONG - THEY DIDN'T PUT UP MUCH OF A FIGHT.

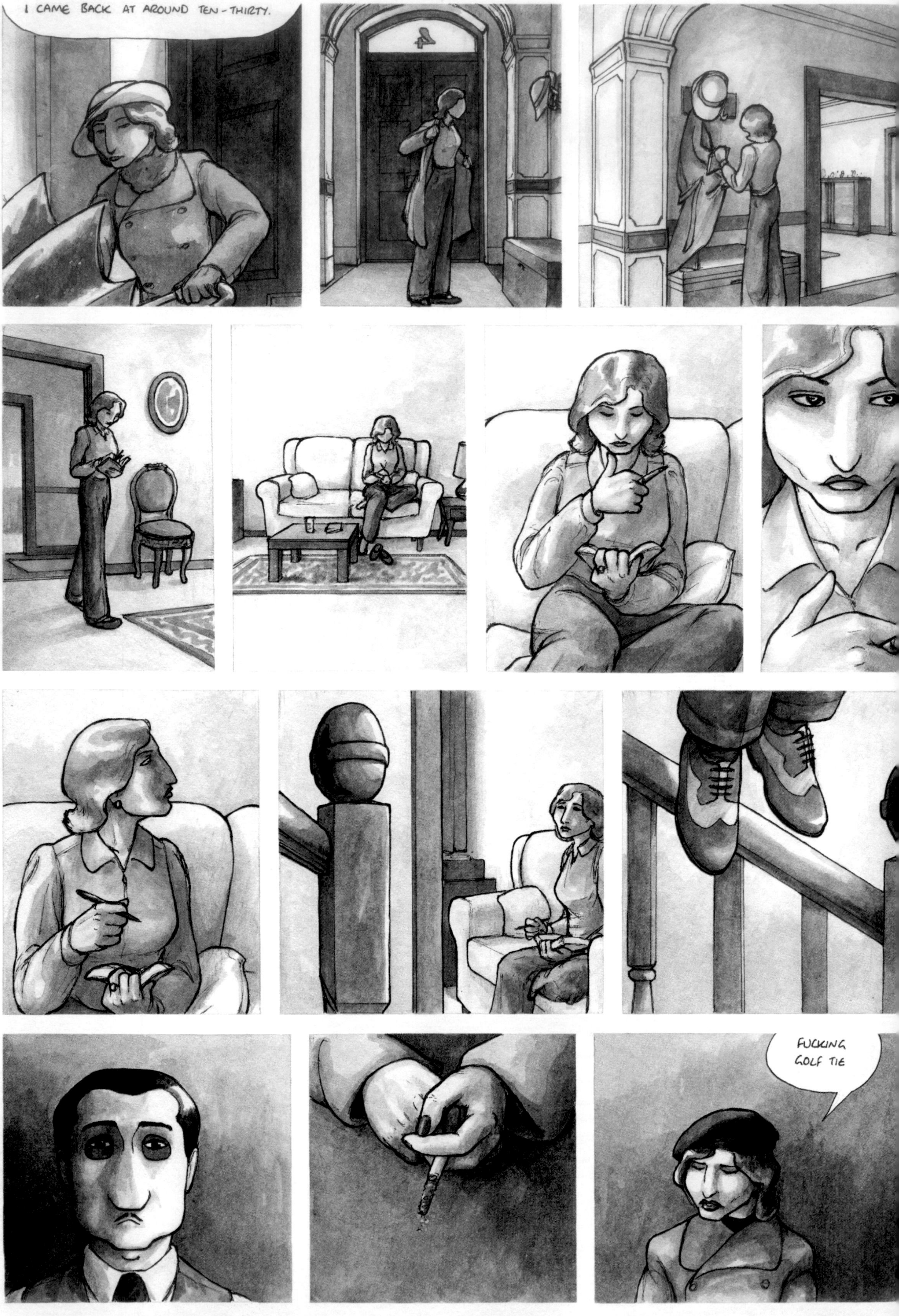
I CAME BACK AT AROUND TEN-THIRTY.
FUCKING GOLF TIE

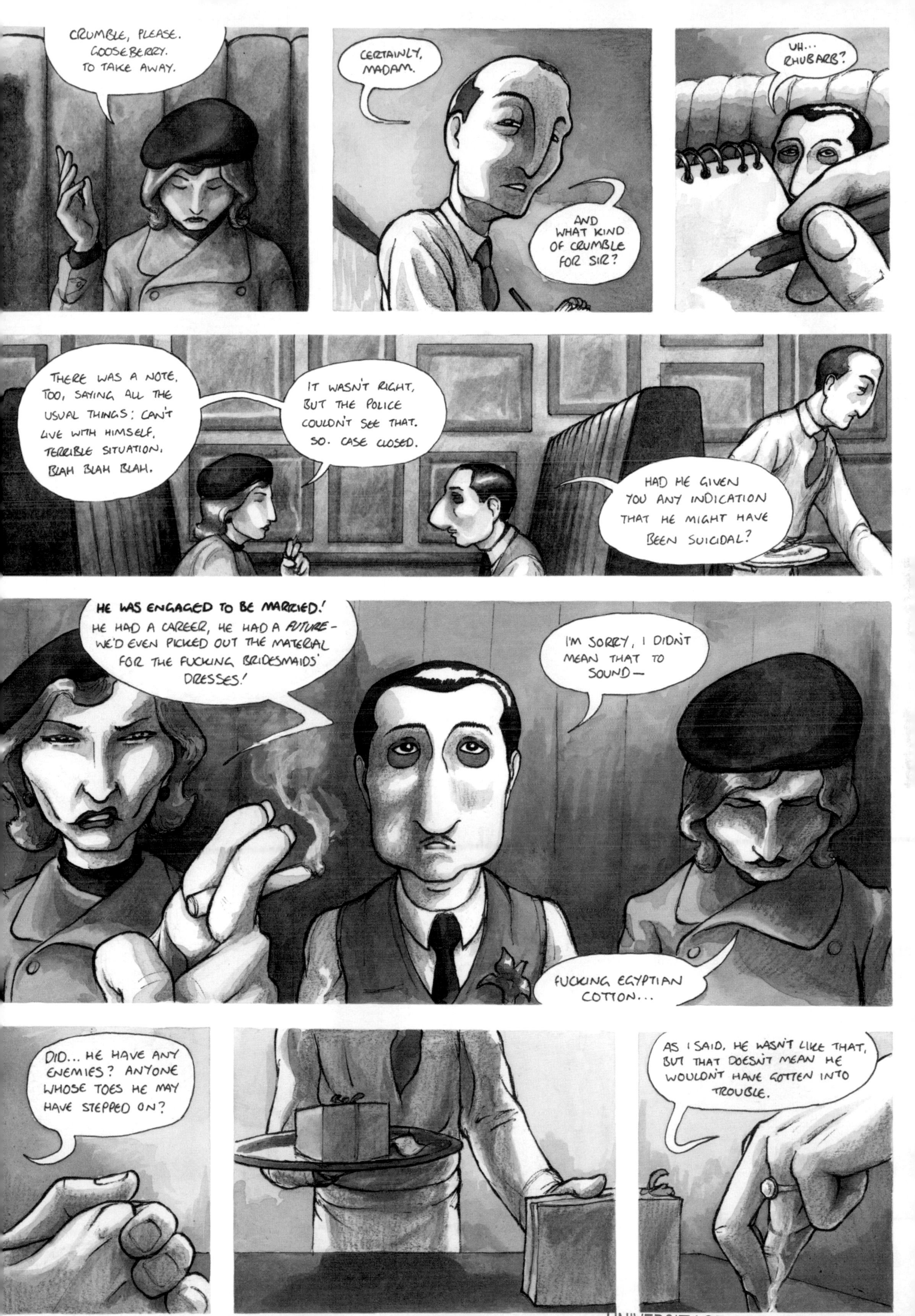
CRUMBLE, PLEASE. GOOSEBERRY. TO TAKE AWAY.
CERTAINLY, MADAM.
AND WHAT KIND OF CRUMBLE FOR SIR?
UH... RHUBARB?
THERE WAS A NOTE, TOO, SAYING ALL THE USUAL THINGS: CAN'T LIVE WITH HIMSELF, TERRIBLE SITUATION, BLAH BLAH BLAH.
IT WASN'T RIGHT, BUT THE POLICE COULDN'T SEE THAT. SO. CASE CLOSED.
HAD HE GIVEN YOU ANY INDICATION THAT HE MIGHT HAVE BEEN SUICIDAL?
HE WAS ENGAGED TO BE MARRIED! HE HAD A CAREER, HE HAD A *FUTURE* - WE'D EVEN PICKED OUT THE MATERIAL FOR THE FUCKING BRIDESMAIDS' DRESSES!
I'M SORRY, I DIDN'T MEAN THAT TO SOUND—
FUCKING EGYPTIAN COTTON...
DID... HE HAVE ANY ENEMIES? ANYONE WHOSE TOES HE MAY HAVE STEPPED ON?
AS I SAID, HE WASN'T LIKE THAT, BUT THAT DOESN'T MEAN HE WOULDN'T HAVE GOTTEN INTO TROUBLE.

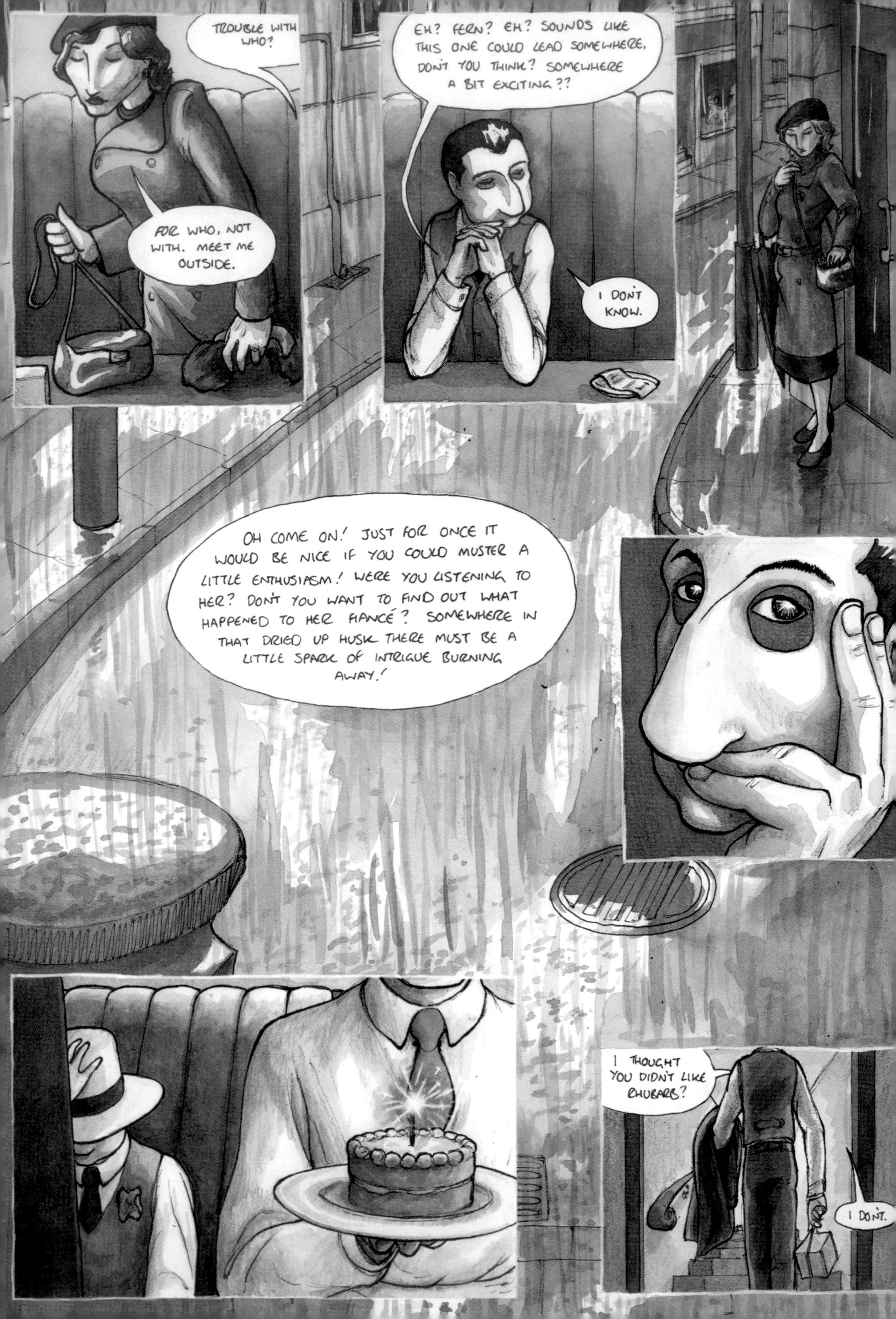
TROUBLE WITH WHO?
FOR WHO, NOT WITH. MEET ME OUTSIDE.
EH? FERN? EH? SOUNDS LIKE THIS ONE COULD LEAD SOMEWHERE, DON'T YOU THINK? SOMEWHERE A BIT EXCITING??
I DON'T KNOW.
OH COME ON! JUST FOR ONCE IT WOULD BE NICE IF YOU COULD MUSTER A LITTLE ENTHUSIASM! WERE YOU LISTENING TO HER? DON'T YOU WANT TO FIND OUT WHAT HAPPENED TO HER FIANCÉ? SOMEWHERE IN THAT DRIED UP HUSK THERE MUST BE A LITTLE SPARK OF INTRIGUE BURNING AWAY!
I THOUGHT YOU DIDN'T LIKE RHUBARB?
I DON'T.

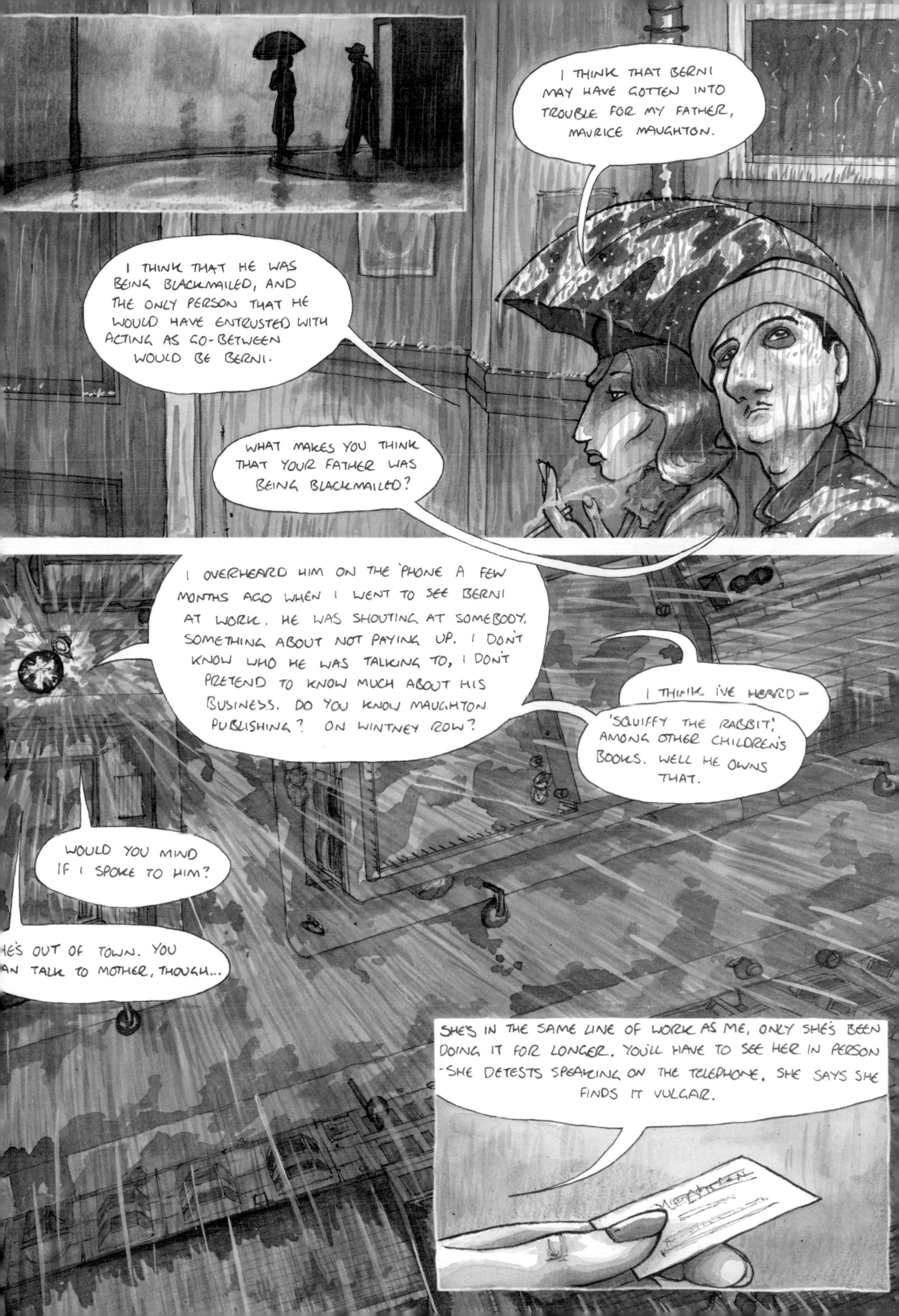
I THINK THAT BERNI MAY HAVE GOTTEN INTO TROUBLE FOR MY FATHER, MAURICE MAUGHTON.
I THINK THAT HE WAS BEING BLACKMAILED, AND THE ONLY PERSON THAT HE WOULD HAVE ENTRUSTED WITH ACTING AS GO-BETWEEN WOULD BE BERNI.
WHAT MAKES YOU THINK THAT YOUR FATHER WAS BEING BLACKMAILED?
I OVERHEARD HIM ON THE 'PHONE A FEW MONTHS AGO WHEN I WENT TO SEE BERNI AT WORK. HE WAS SHOUTING AT SOMEBODY, SOMETHING ABOUT NOT PAYING UP. I DON'T KNOW WHO HE WAS TALKING TO, I DON'T PRETEND TO KNOW MUCH ABOUT HIS BUSINESS. DO YOU KNOW MAUGHTON PUBLISHING? ON WINTNEY ROW?
I THINK I'VE HEARD—
'SQUIFFY THE RABBIT', AMONG OTHER CHILDREN'S BOOKS. WELL HE OWNS THAT.
WOULD YOU MIND IF I SPOKE TO HIM?
HE'S OUT OF TOWN. YOU CAN TALK TO MOTHER, THOUGH...
SHE'S IN THE SAME LINE OF WORK AS ME, ONLY SHE'S BEEN DOING IT FOR LONGER. YOU'LL HAVE TO SEE HER IN PERSON - SHE DETESTS SPEAKING ON THE TELEPHONE. SHE SAYS SHE FINDS IT VULGAR.

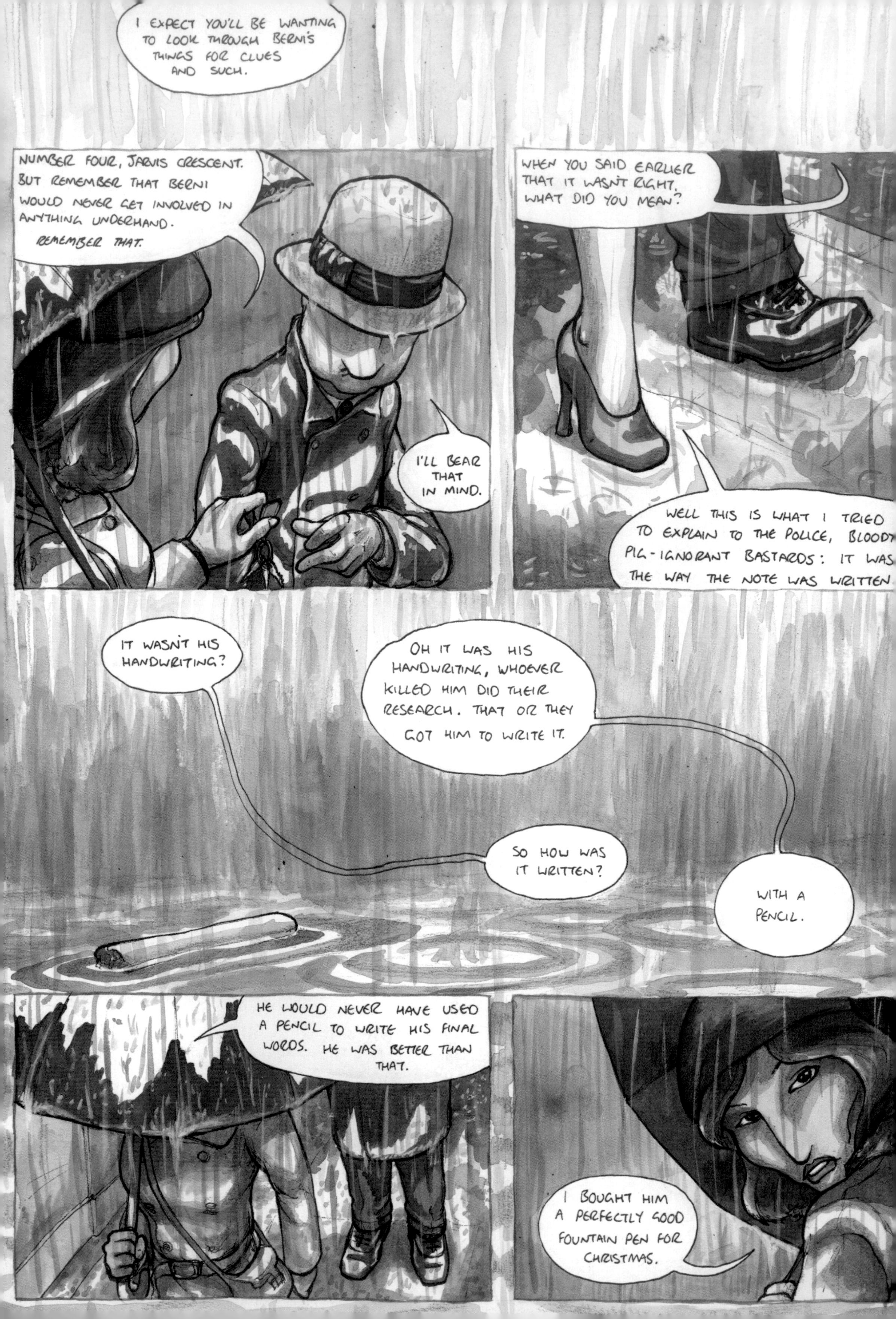
I EXPECT YOU'LL BE WANTING TO LOOK THROUGH BERNI'S THINGS FOR CLUES AND SUCH.
NUMBER FOUR, JARVIS CRESCENT. BUT REMEMBER THAT BERNI WOULD NEVER GET INVOLVED IN ANYTHING UNDERHAND. REMEMBER THAT.
I'LL BEAR THAT IN MIND.
WHEN YOU SAID EARLIER THAT IT WASN'T RIGHT, WHAT DID YOU MEAN?
WELL THIS IS WHAT I TRIED TO EXPLAIN TO THE POLICE, BLOODY PIG-IGNORANT BASTARDS: IT WAS THE WAY THE NOTE WAS WRITTEN.
IT WASN'T HIS HANDWRITING?
OH IT WAS HIS HANDWRITING, WHOEVER KILLED HIM DID THEIR RESEARCH. THAT OR THEY GOT HIM TO WRITE IT.
SO HOW WAS IT WRITTEN?
WITH A PENCIL.
HE WOULD NEVER HAVE USED A PENCIL TO WRITE HIS FINAL WORDS. HE WAS BETTER THAN THAT.
I BOUGHT HIM A PERFECTLY GOOD FOUNTAIN PEN FOR CHRISTMAS.

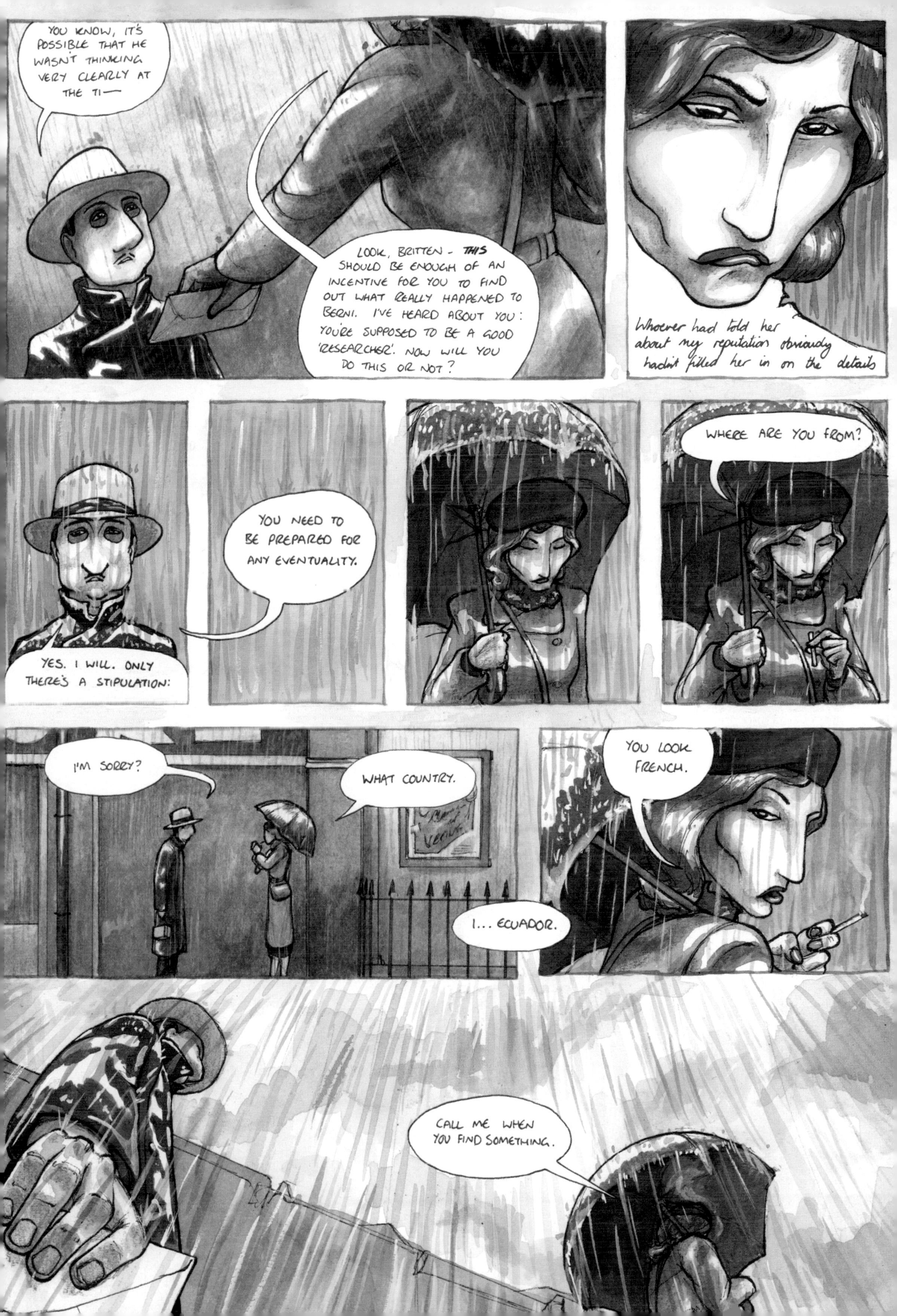
YOU KNOW, IT'S POSSIBLE THAT HE WASN'T THINKING VERY CLEARLY AT THE TI—
LOOK, BRITTEN - THIS SHOULD BE ENOUGH OF AN INCENTIVE FOR YOU TO FIND OUT WHAT REALLY HAPPENED TO BERNI. I'VE HEARD ABOUT YOU: YOU'RE SUPPOSED TO BE A GOOD 'RESEARCHER'. NOW WILL YOU DO THIS OR NOT?
Whoever had told her about my reputation obviously hadn't filled her in on the details
YES. I WILL. ONLY THERE'S A STIPULATION:
YOU NEED TO BE PREPARED FOR ANY EVENTUALITY.
WHERE ARE YOU FROM?
I'M SORRY?
WHAT COUNTRY.
YOU LOOK FRENCH.
I... ECUADOR.
CALL ME WHEN YOU FIND SOMETHING.

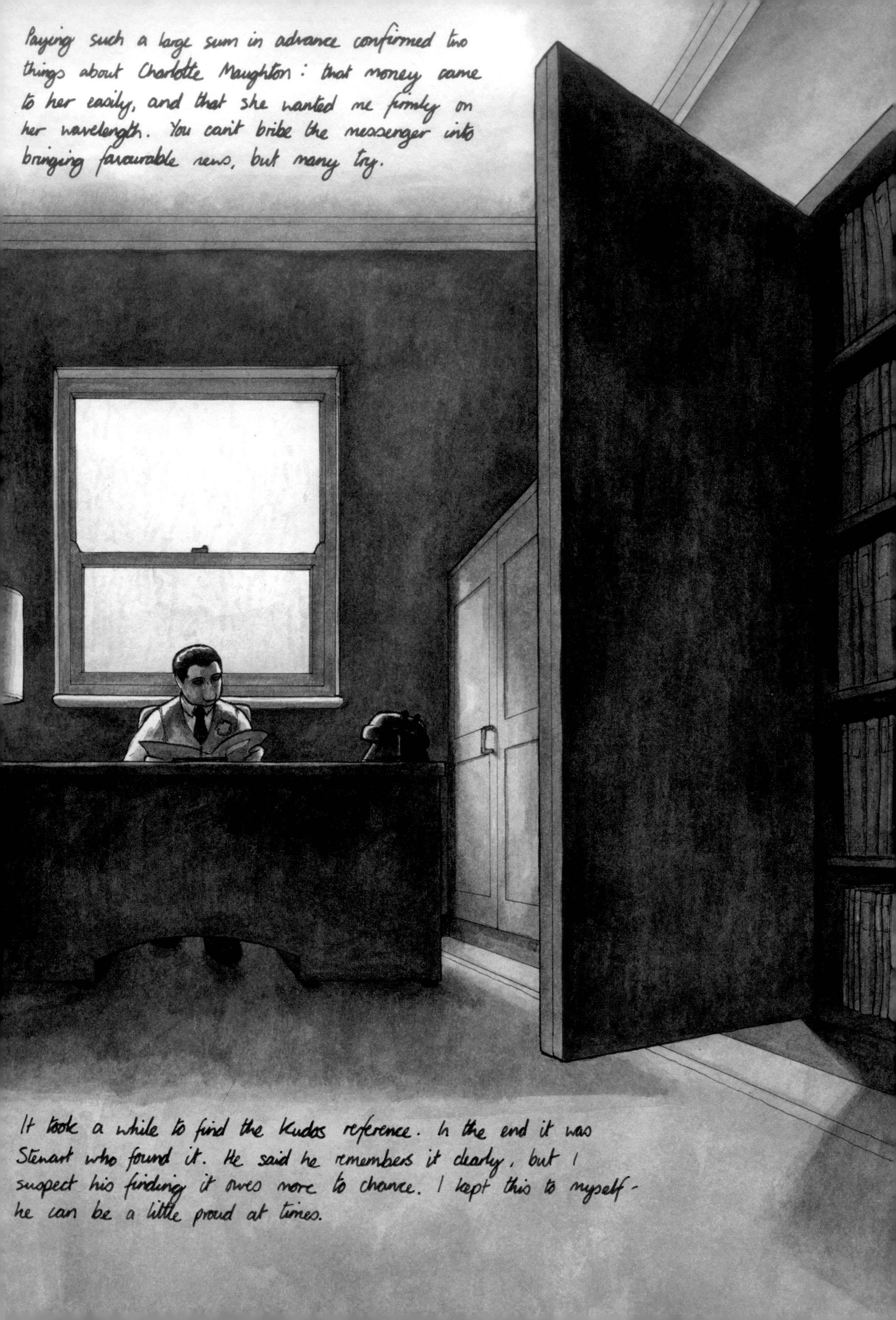
Paying such a large sum in advance confirmed two things about Charlotte Maughton: that money came to her easily, and that she wanted me firmly on her wavelength. You can't bribe the messenger into bringing favourable news, but many try.
It took a while to find the Kudos reference. In the end it was Stewart who found it. He said he remembers it clearly, but I suspect his finding it owes more to chance. I kept this to myself - he can be a little proud at times.

Regularly out-of-town solicitor Mr Gregory Murch had become concerned about Mrs Frances Murch's increasingly distant and distracted disposition. He was reluctant to suspect an affair, but not too reluctant to hire someone to try and prove it. It was the usual case of paranoia dressed up in marital concern.

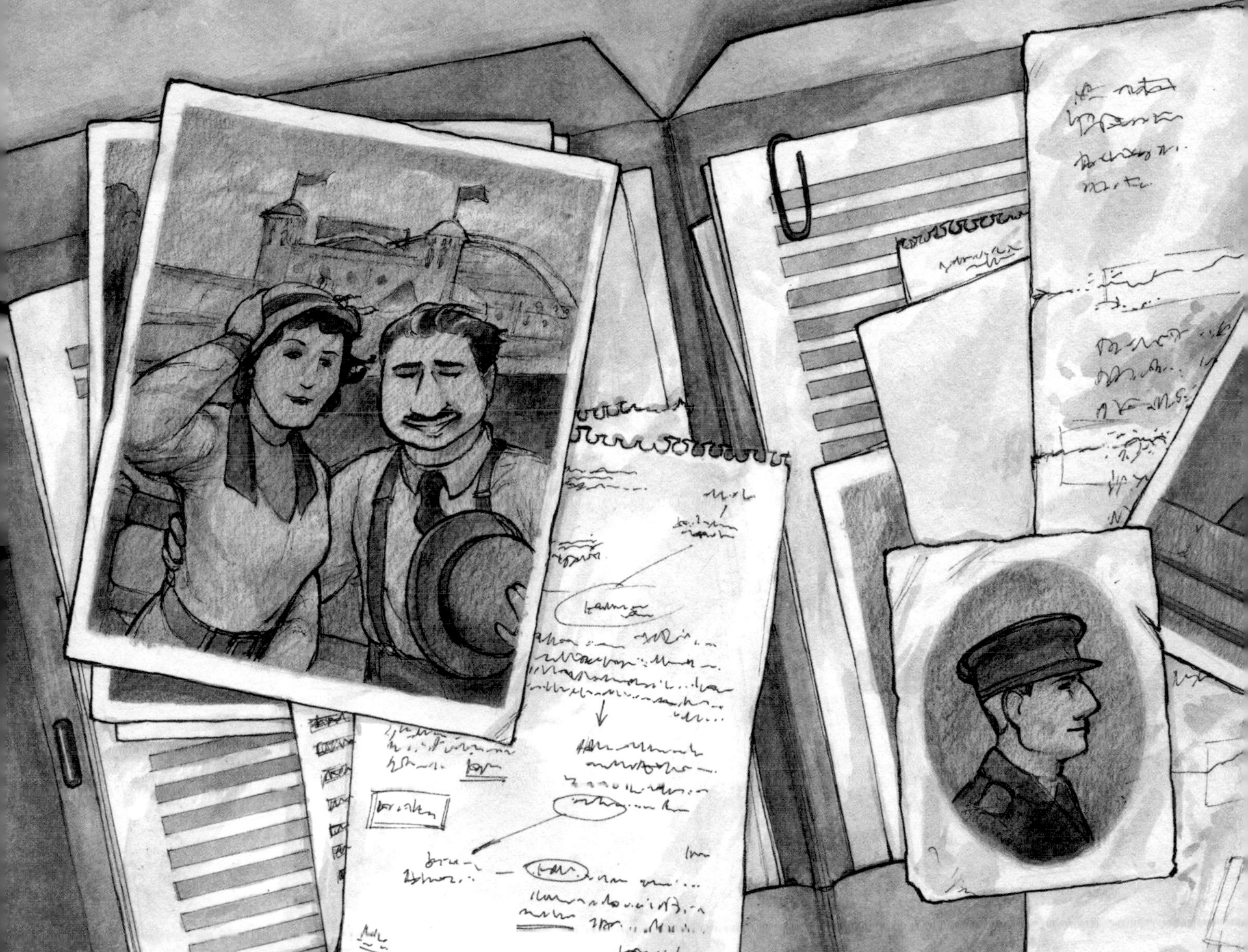

I'd followed her around until I was satisfied there was nothing for the husband to be concerned about. However, while digging a little into the wife's history. I discovered that she hadn't always been so faithful. Many years before, Gregory had been busy travelling back and forth settling the estate of a deceased client, and Frances had been busy with a dashing young serviceman. In fact, during one of Gregory's trips away, she had fallen pregnant with the child of this dashing young serviceman. The dashing young serviceman in question was Michael Kudos – Bernie's brother.

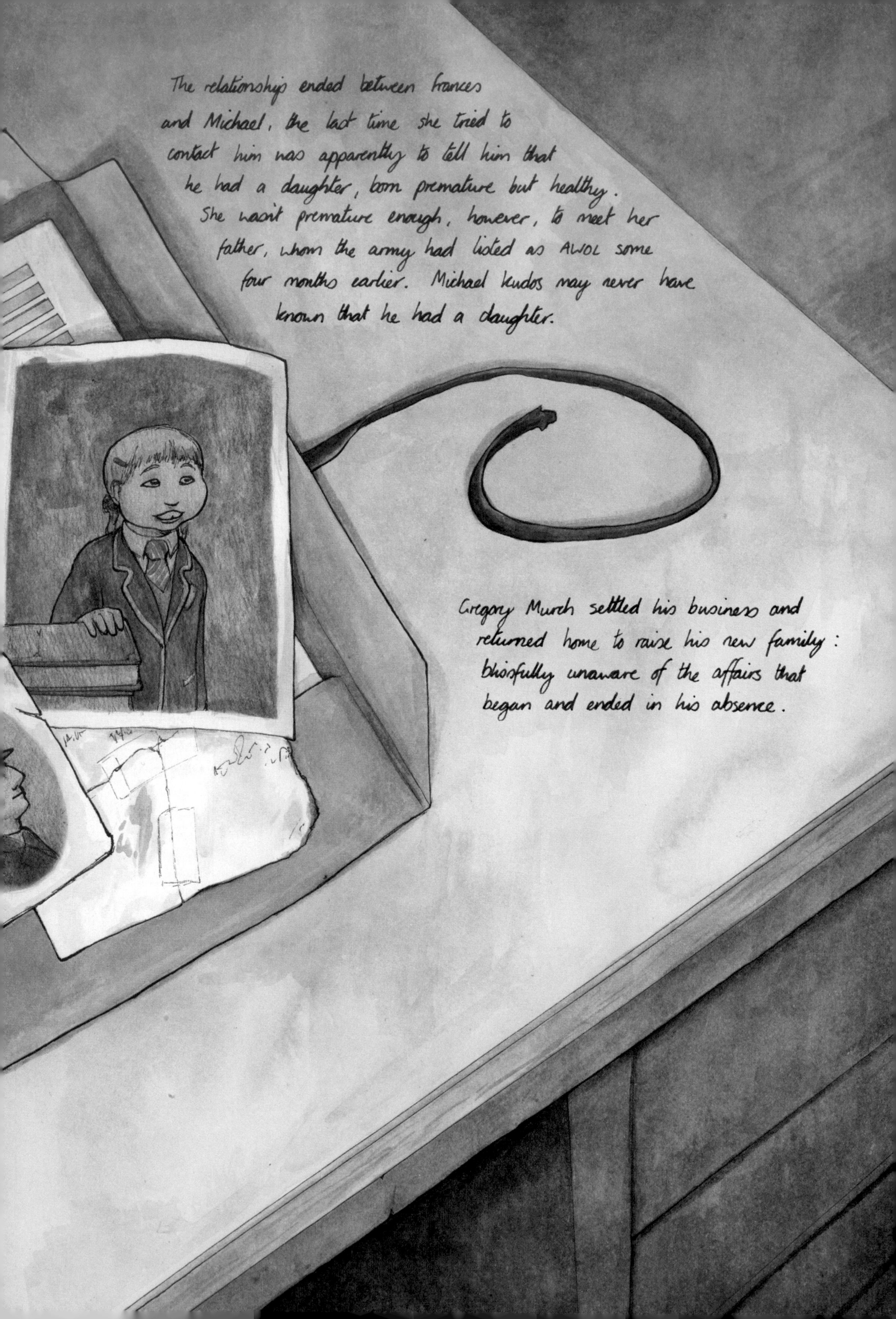
The relationship ended between Frances and Michael, the last time she tried to contact him was apparently to tell him that he had a daughter, born premature but healthy. She wasn't premature enough, however, to meet her father, whom the army had listed as AWOL some four months earlier. Michael Kudos may never have known that he had a daughter.
Gregory Murch settled his business and returned home to raise his new family: blissfully unaware of the affairs that began and ended in his absence.

Even with the file, I was struggling to remember Gregory Murch. I told this man that his beloved daughter, Lenora, was another man's child, but I don't recall what his reaction was. I don't even remember if he cried or not. After a while, every bombshell looks just like the next.

I could see how the thought of revenge might still burn angrily, but to kill the brother of the man responsible after so many years was quite a stretch.

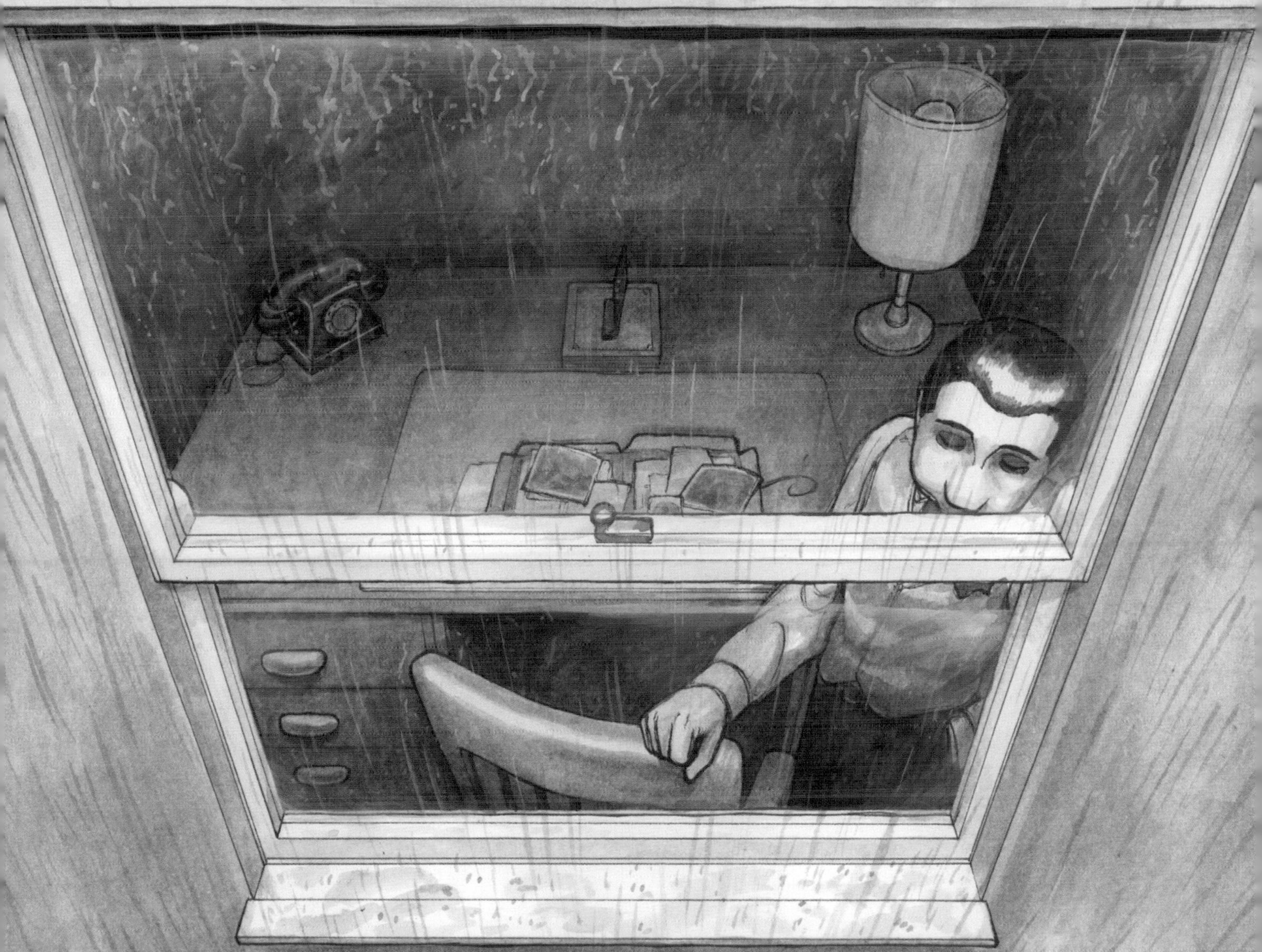

I needed to know more about Bemi Kudos.

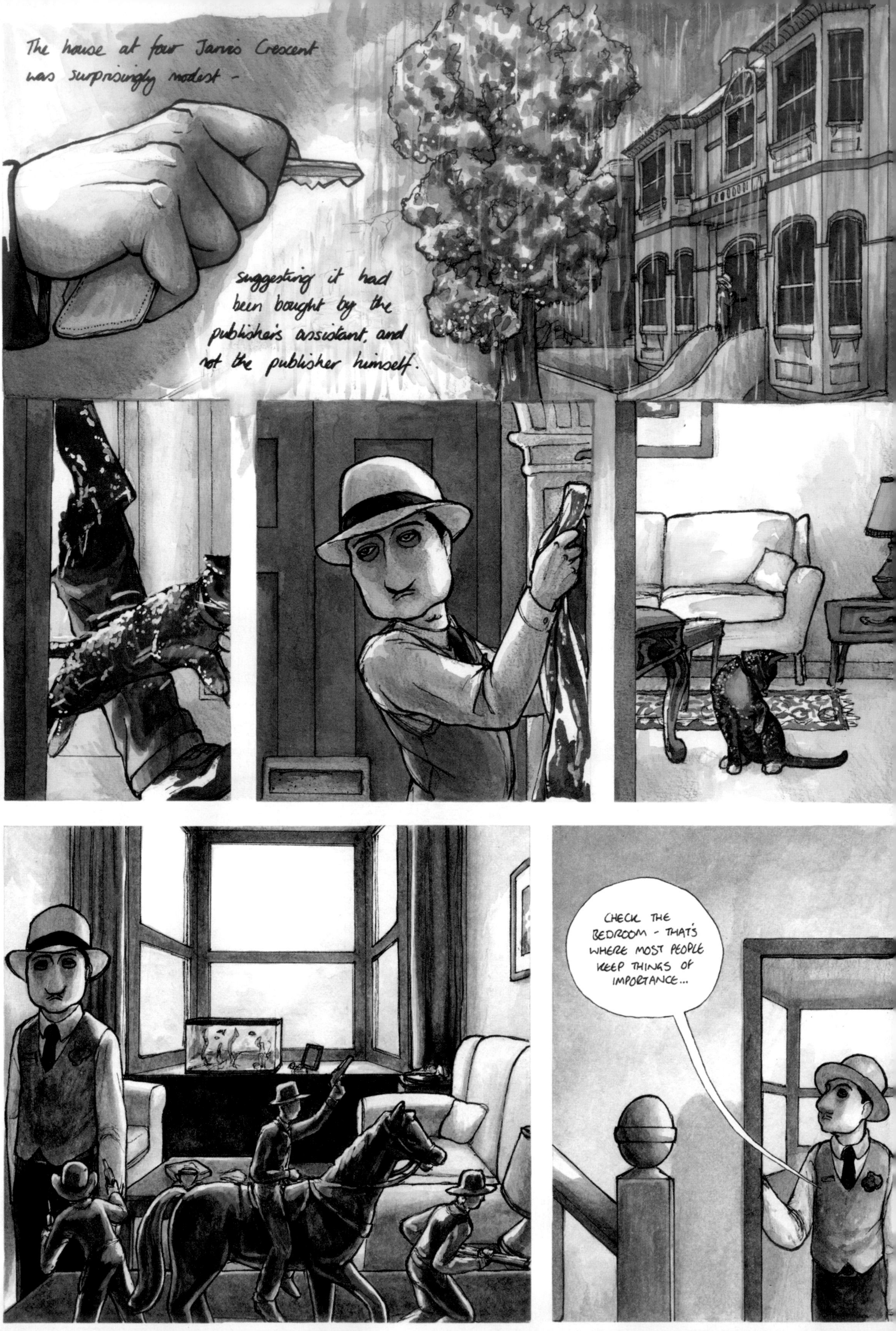
The house at four Jarvis Crescent was surprisingly modest -
suggesting it had been bought by the publisher's assistant, and not the publisher himself.
CHECK THE BEDROOM - THAT'S WHERE MOST PEOPLE KEEP THINGS OF IMPORTANCE...

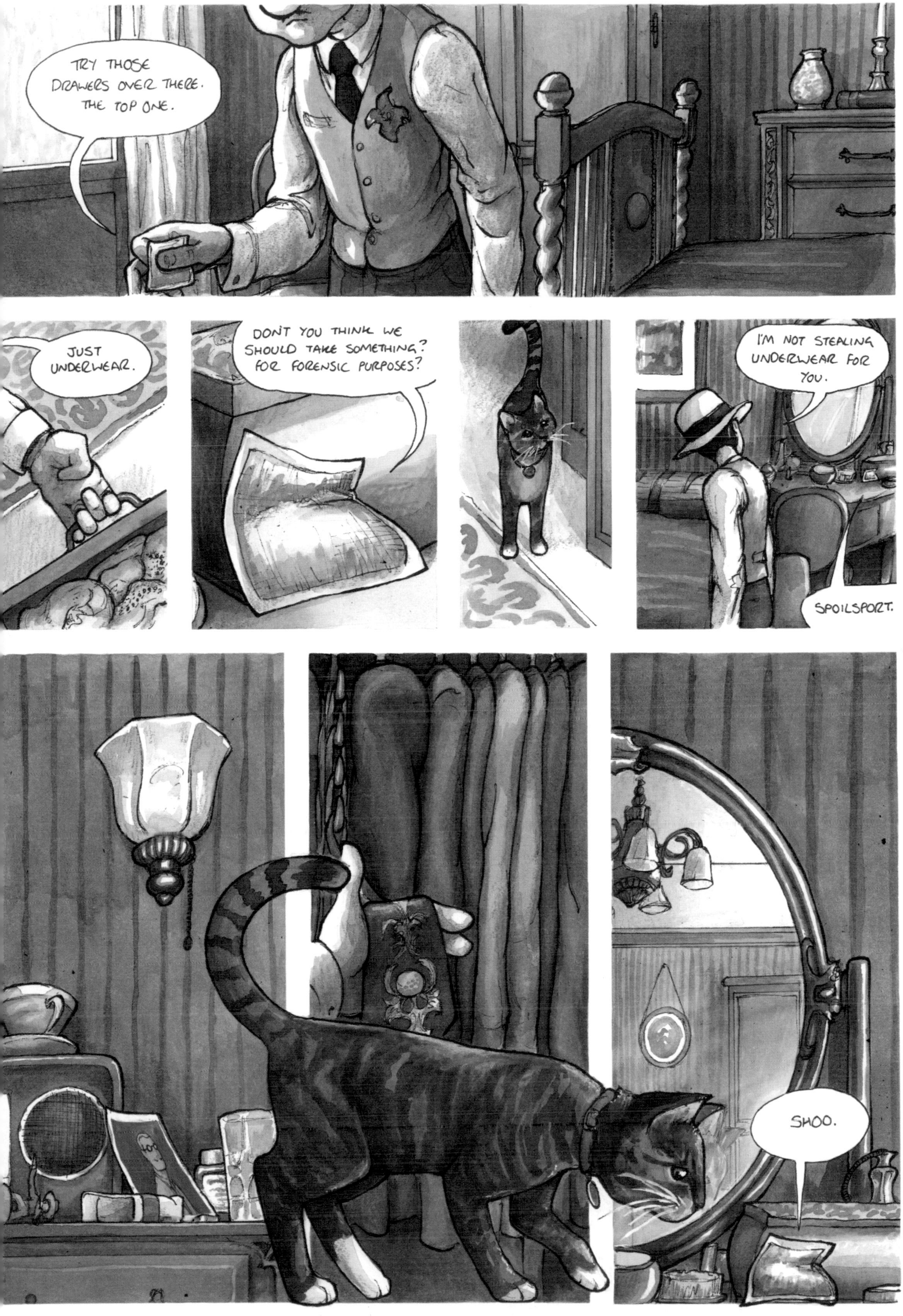
TRY THOSE DRAWERS OVER THERE. THE TOP ONE.
JUST UNDERWEAR.
DON'T YOU THINK WE SHOULD TAKE SOMETHING? FOR FORENSIC PURPOSES?
I'M NOT STEALING UNDERWEAR FOR YOU.
SPOILSPORT.
SHOO.

I was slowly building a profile of Berni from the rest of materiality he had created during the last years of his life.

It wasn't comprehensive:

it didn't tell me his state of mind, or his worries, or his delusions, or his ambitions,

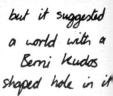

but it suggested a world with a Berni Kudos shaped hole in it

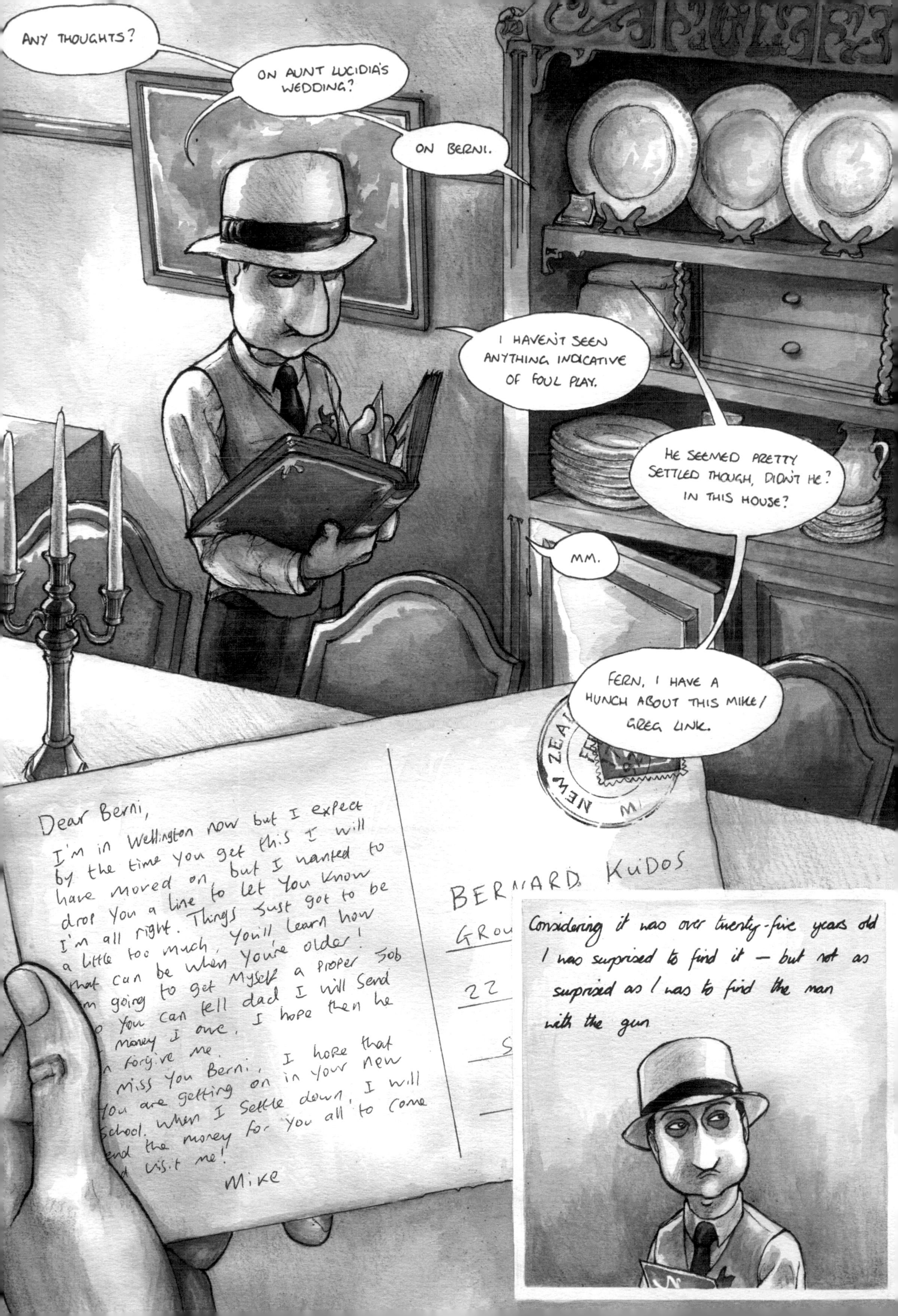
ANY THOUGHTS?
ON AUNT LUCIDIA'S WEDDING?
ON BERNI.
I HAVEN'T SEEN ANYTHING INDICATIVE OF FOUL PLAY.
HE SEEMED PRETTY SETTLED THOUGH, DIDN'T HE? IN THIS HOUSE?
MM.
FERN, I HAVE A HUNCH ABOUT THIS MIKE/ GREG LINK.
Dear Berni,
I'm in Wellington now but I expect
by the time you get this I will
have moved on, but I wanted to
drop you a line to let you know
I'm all right. Things just got to be
a little too much, you'll learn how
hat can be when you're older!
m going to get myself a proper job
o you can tell dad I will send
money I owe, I hope then he
n forgive me.
miss you Berni, I hope that
ou are getting on in your new
School. When I settle down, I will
end the money for you all to come
visit me!
Mike
BERNARD KUDOS
GROU
22
S
Considering it was over twenty-five years old I was surprised to find it – but not as surprised as I was to find the man with the gun

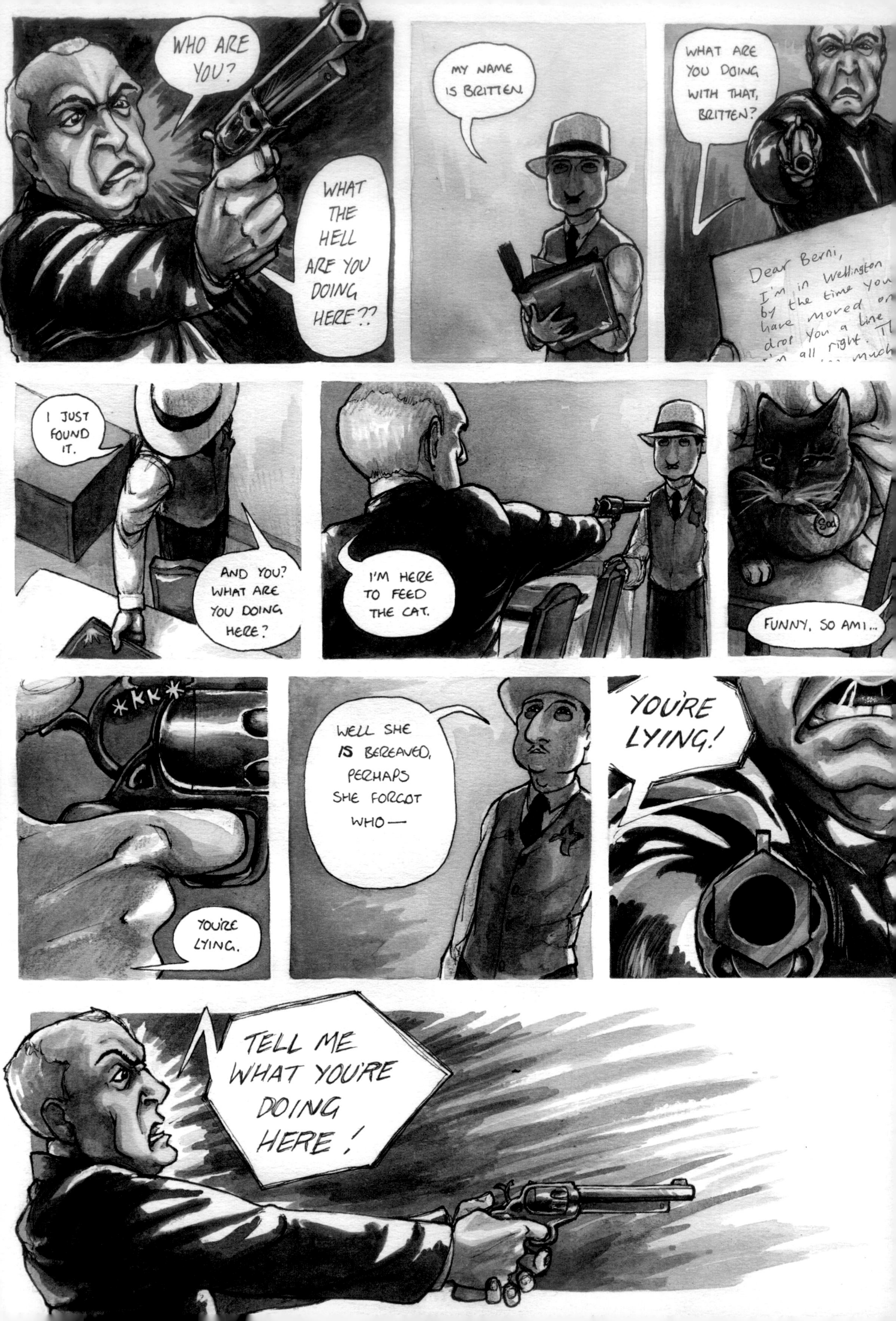
WHO ARE YOU?
WHAT THE HELL ARE YOU DOING HERE??
MY NAME IS BRITTEN.
WHAT ARE YOU DOING WITH THAT, BRITTEN?
Dear Berni,
I'm in Wellington
by the time you
have moved on
drop you a line.
I JUST FOUND IT.
AND YOU? WHAT ARE YOU DOING HERE?
I'M HERE TO FEED THE CAT.
FUNNY, SO AM I...
KK
YOU'RE LYING.
WELL SHE **IS** BEREAVED, PERHAPS SHE FORGOT WHO—
YOU'RE LYING!
TELL ME WHAT YOU'RE DOING HERE!

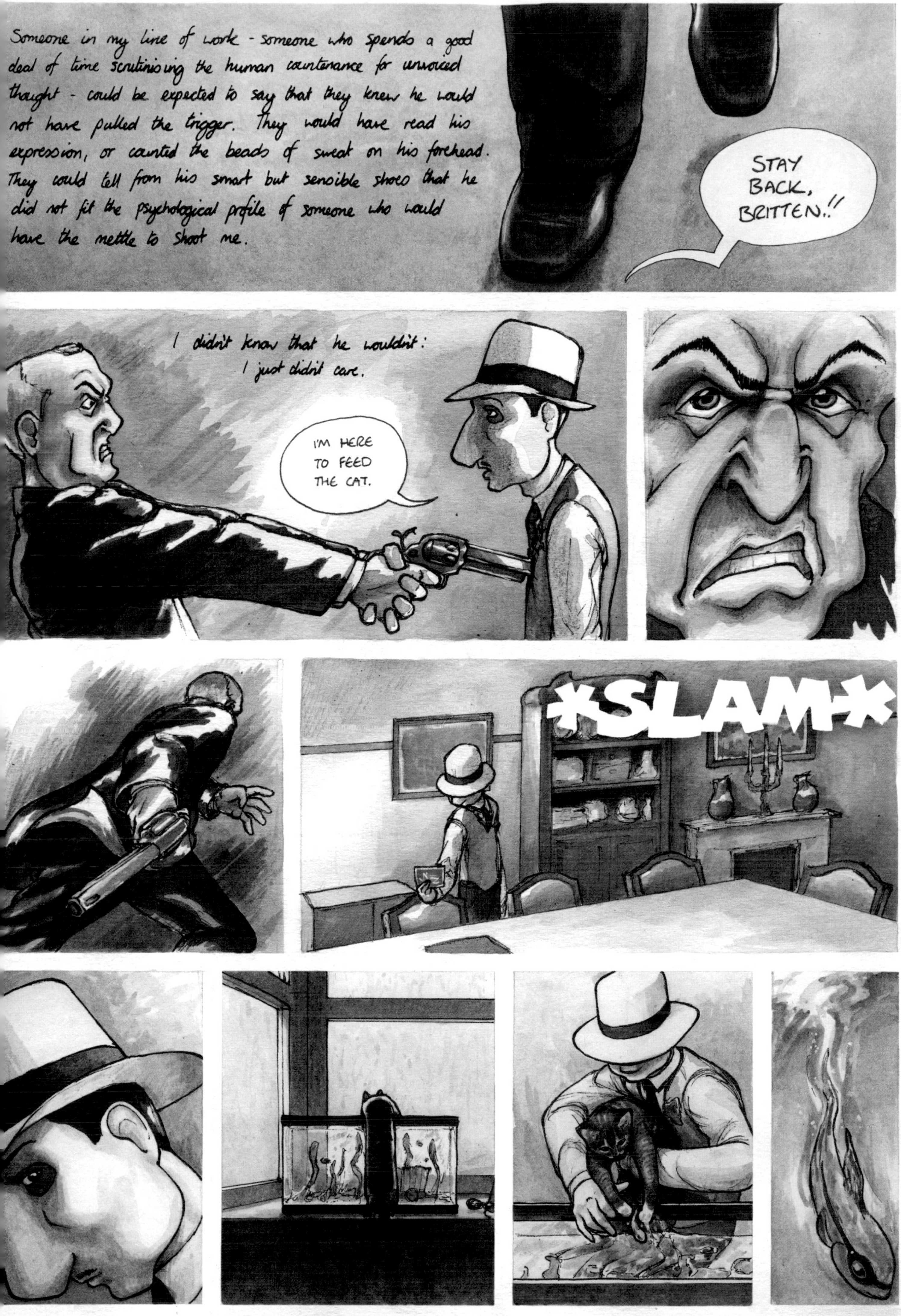
Someone in my line of work - someone who spends a good deal of time scrutinising the human countenance for unvoiced thought - could be expected to say that they knew he would not have pulled the trigger. They would have read his expression, or counted the beads of sweat on his forehead. They could tell from his smart but sensible shoes that he did not fit the psychological profile of someone who would have the mettle to shoot me.
STAY BACK, BRITTEN.!!
I didn't know that he wouldn't:
I just didn't care.
I'M HERE TO FEED THE CAT.
SLAM

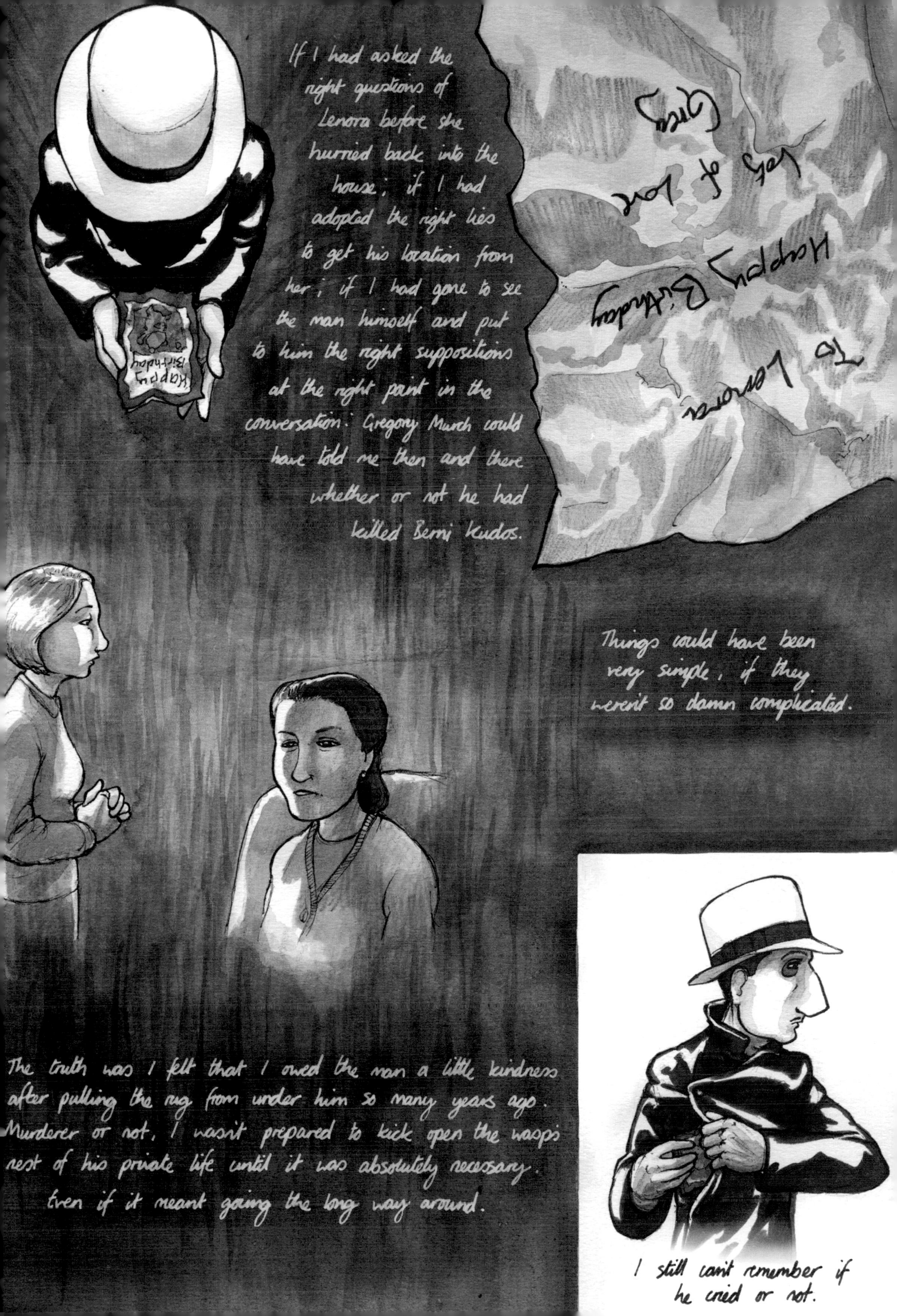
If I had asked the right questions of Lenora before she hurried back into the house; if I had adopted the right lies to get his location from her; if I had gone to see the man himself and put to him the right suppositions at the right point in the conversation: Gregory March could have told me then and there whether or not he had killed Berni Kudos.
Happy Birthday
To Lenora
Happy Birthday
lots of love
Greg
Things could have been very simple, if they weren't so damn complicated.
The truth was I felt that I owed the man a little kindness after pulling the rug from under him so many years ago. Murderer or not, I wasn't prepared to kick open the wasps' nest of his private life until it was absolutely necessary. Even if it meant going the long way around.
I still can't remember if he cried or not.

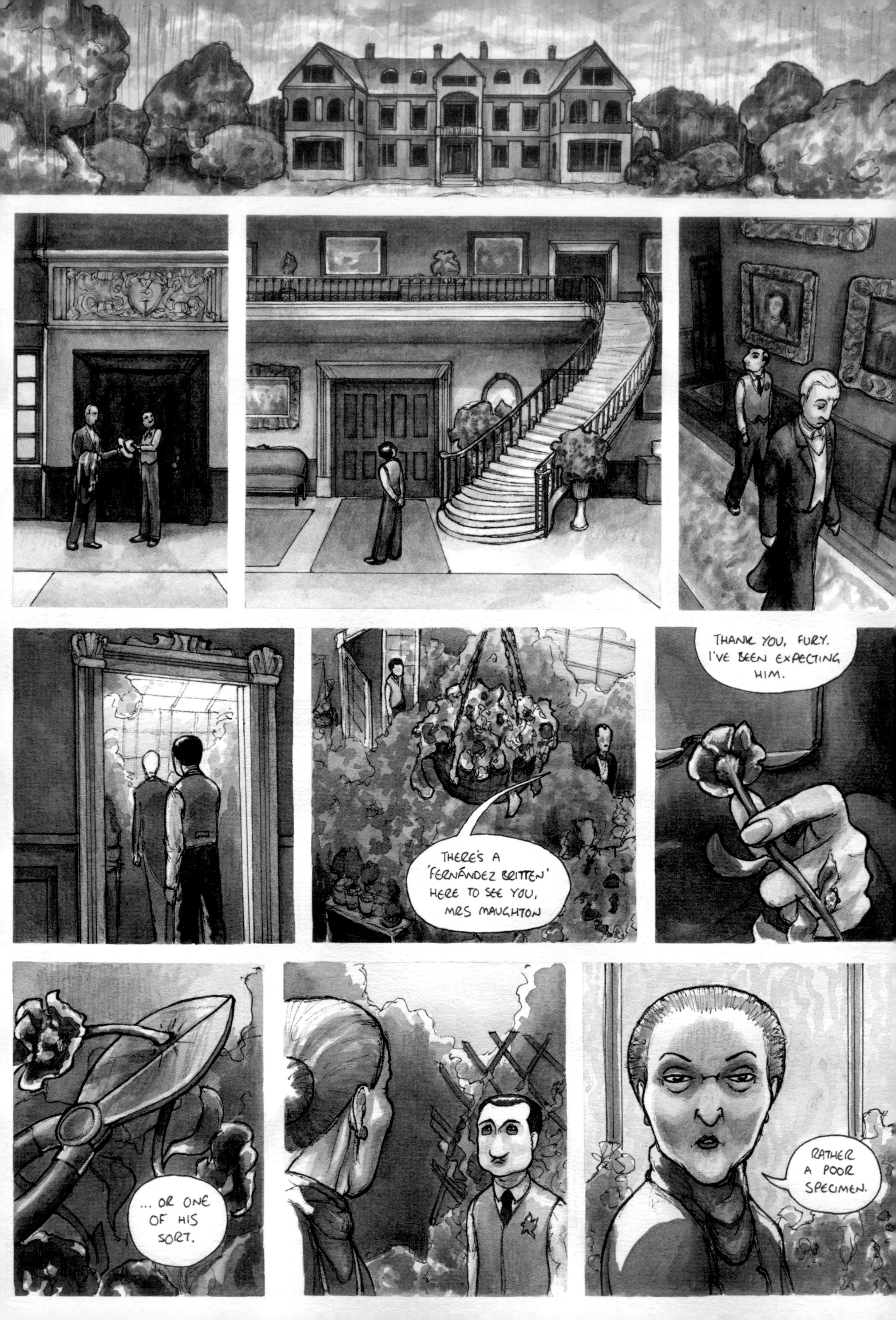
THERE'S A 'FERNÁNDEZ BRITTEN' HERE TO SEE YOU, MRS MAUGHTON
THANK YOU, FURY. I'VE BEEN EXPECTING HIM.
... OR ONE OF HIS SORT.
RATHER A POOR SPECIMEN.

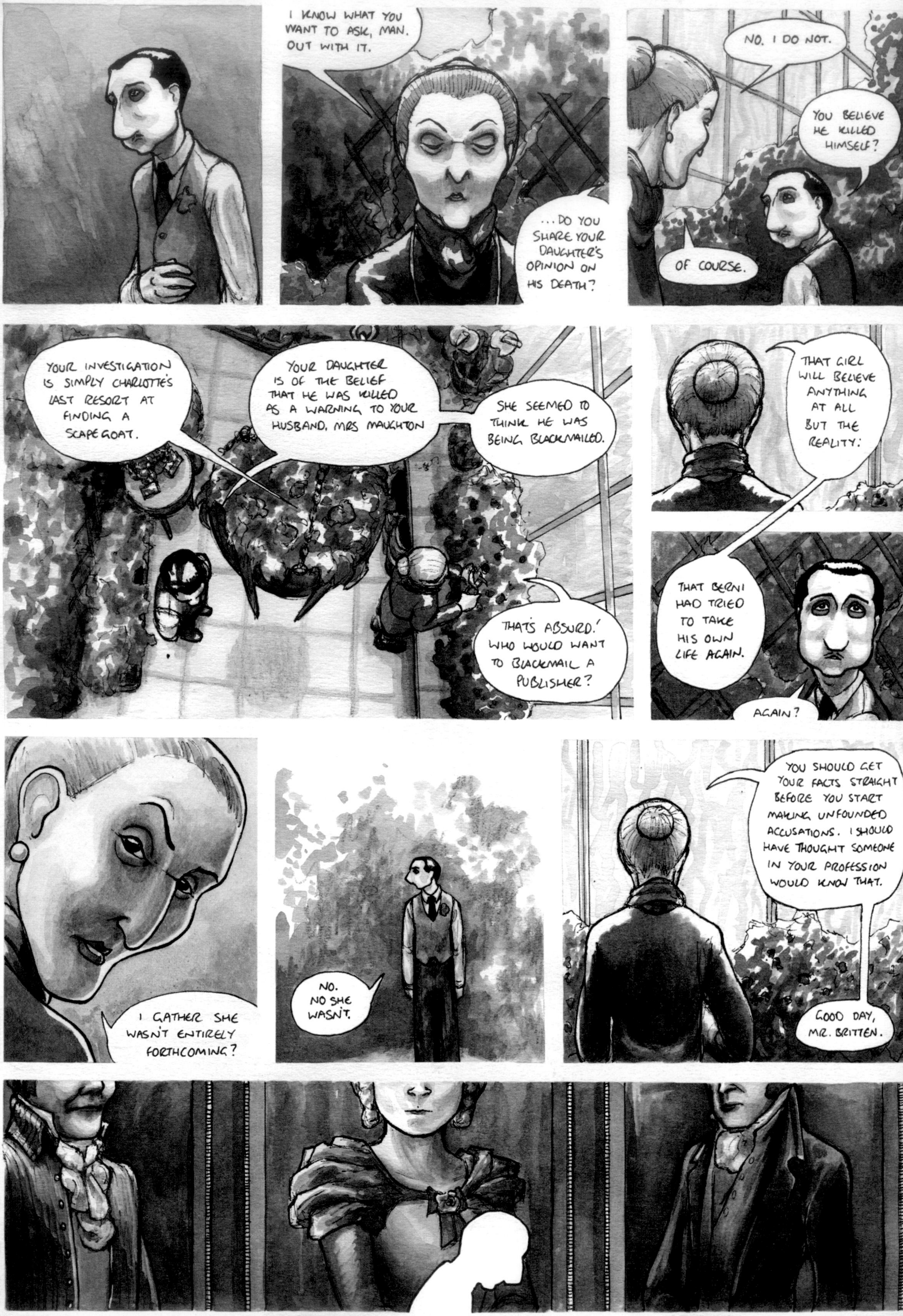
I KNOW WHAT YOU WANT TO ASK, MAN. OUT WITH IT.
...DO YOU SHARE YOUR DAUGHTER'S OPINION ON HIS DEATH?
NO, I DO NOT.
YOU BELIEVE HE KILLED HIMSELF?
OF COURSE.
YOUR INVESTIGATION IS SIMPLY CHARLOTTE'S LAST RESORT AT FINDING A SCAPEGOAT.
YOUR DAUGHTER IS OF THE BELIEF THAT HE WAS KILLED AS A WARNING TO YOUR HUSBAND, MRS MAUGHTON
SHE SEEMED TO THINK HE WAS BEING BLACKMAILED.
THAT'S ABSURD! WHO WOULD WANT TO BLACKMAIL A PUBLISHER?
THAT GIRL WILL BELIEVE ANYTHING AT ALL BUT THE REALITY:
THAT BERNI HAD TRIED TO TAKE HIS OWN LIFE AGAIN.
AGAIN?
I GATHER SHE WASN'T ENTIRELY FORTHCOMING?
NO. NO SHE WASN'T.
YOU SHOULD GET YOUR FACTS STRAIGHT BEFORE YOU START MAKING UNFOUNDED ACCUSATIONS. I SHOULD HAVE THOUGHT SOMEONE IN YOUR PROFESSION WOULD KNOW THAT.
GOOD DAY, MR. BRITTEN.

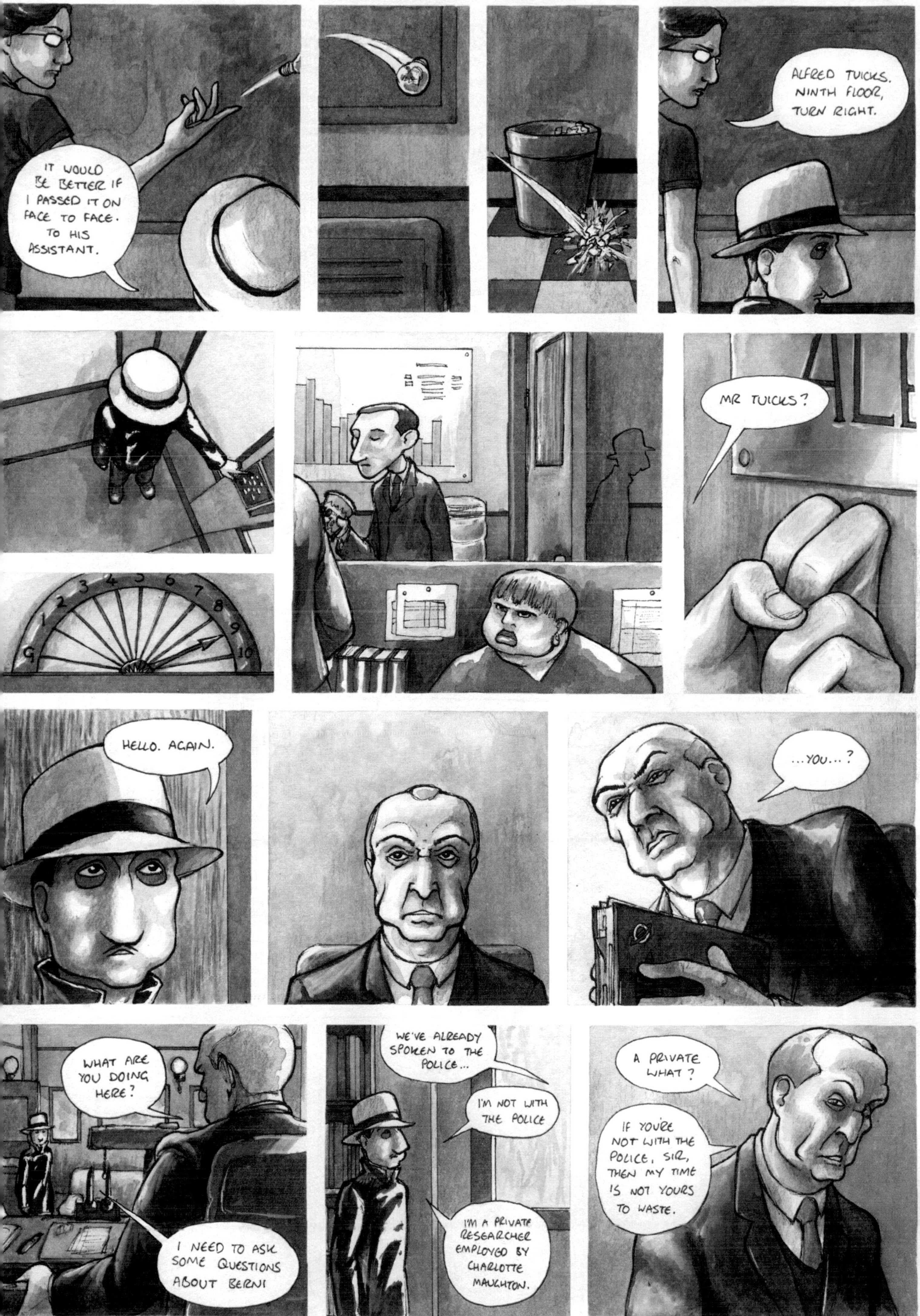
IT WOULD BE BETTER IF I PASSED IT ON FACE TO FACE. TO HIS ASSISTANT.
ALFRED TUICKS. NINTH FLOOR, TURN RIGHT.
G 1 2 3 4 5 6 7 8 9 10
MR TUICKS?
ALE
HELLO. AGAIN.
...YOU...?
WHAT ARE YOU DOING HERE?
I NEED TO ASK SOME QUESTIONS ABOUT BERNI
WE'VE ALREADY SPOKEN TO THE POLICE...
I'M NOT WITH THE POLICE
I'M A PRIVATE RESEARCHER EMPLOYED BY CHARLOTTE MAUGHTON.
A PRIVATE WHAT?
IF YOU'RE NOT WITH THE POLICE, SIR, THEN MY TIME IS NOT YOURS TO WASTE.

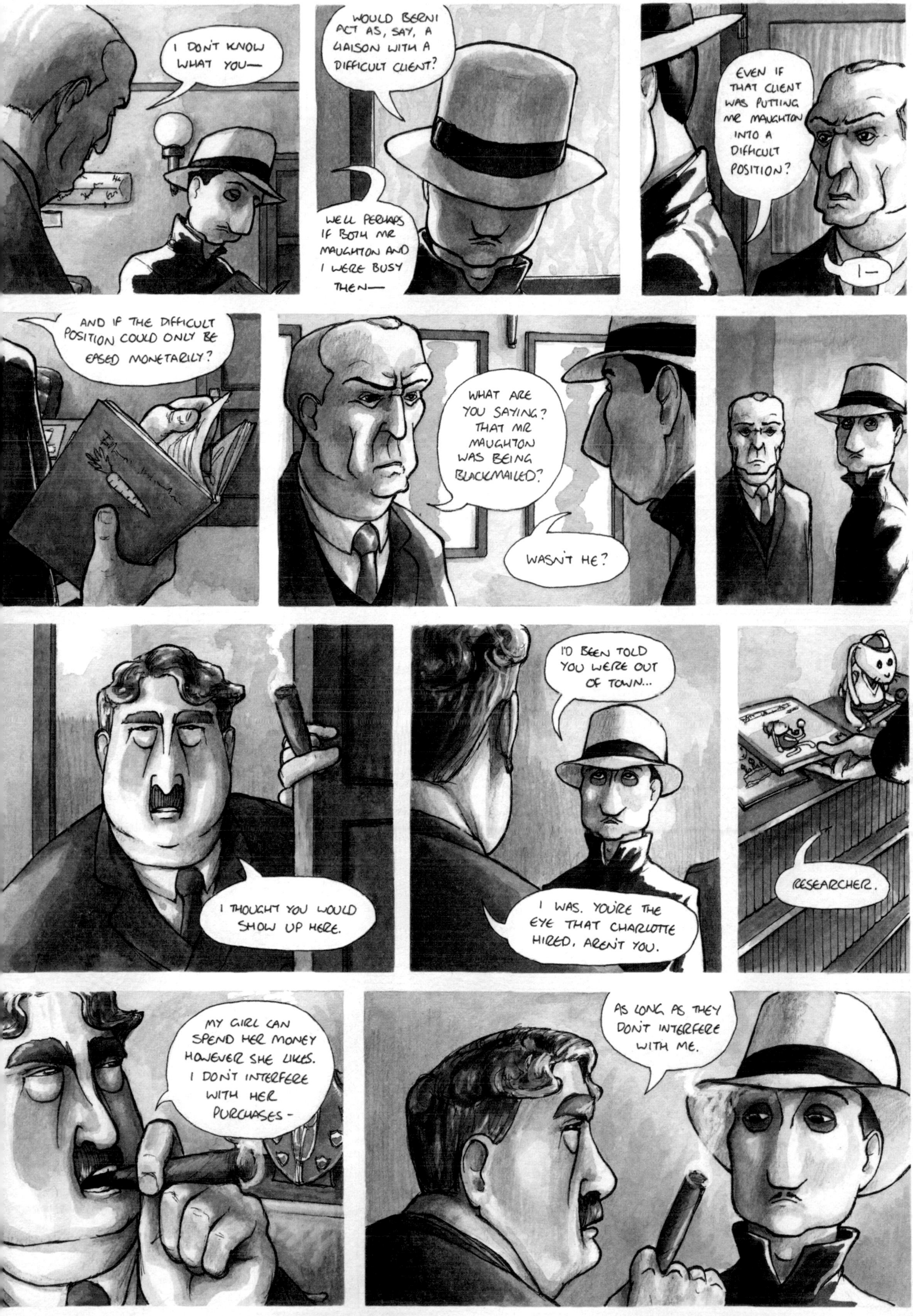

I DON'T KNOW WHAT YOU—
WOULD BERNI ACT AS, SAY, A LIAISON WITH A DIFFICULT CLIENT?
WELL PERHAPS IF BOTH MR MAUGHTON AND I WERE BUSY THEN—
EVEN IF THAT CLIENT WAS PUTTING MR MAUGHTON INTO A DIFFICULT POSITION?
I—
AND IF THE DIFFICULT POSITION COULD ONLY BE EASED MONETARILY?
WHAT ARE YOU SAYING? THAT MR MAUGHTON WAS BEING BLACKMAILED?
WASN'T HE?
I THOUGHT YOU WOULD SHOW UP HERE.
I'D BEEN TOLD YOU WERE OUT OF TOWN...
I WAS. YOU'RE THE EYE THAT CHARLOTTE HIRED, AREN'T YOU.
RESEARCHER.
MY GIRL CAN SPEND HER MONEY HOWEVER SHE LIKES. I DON'T INTERFERE WITH HER PURCHASES-
AS LONG AS THEY DON'T INTERFERE WITH ME.

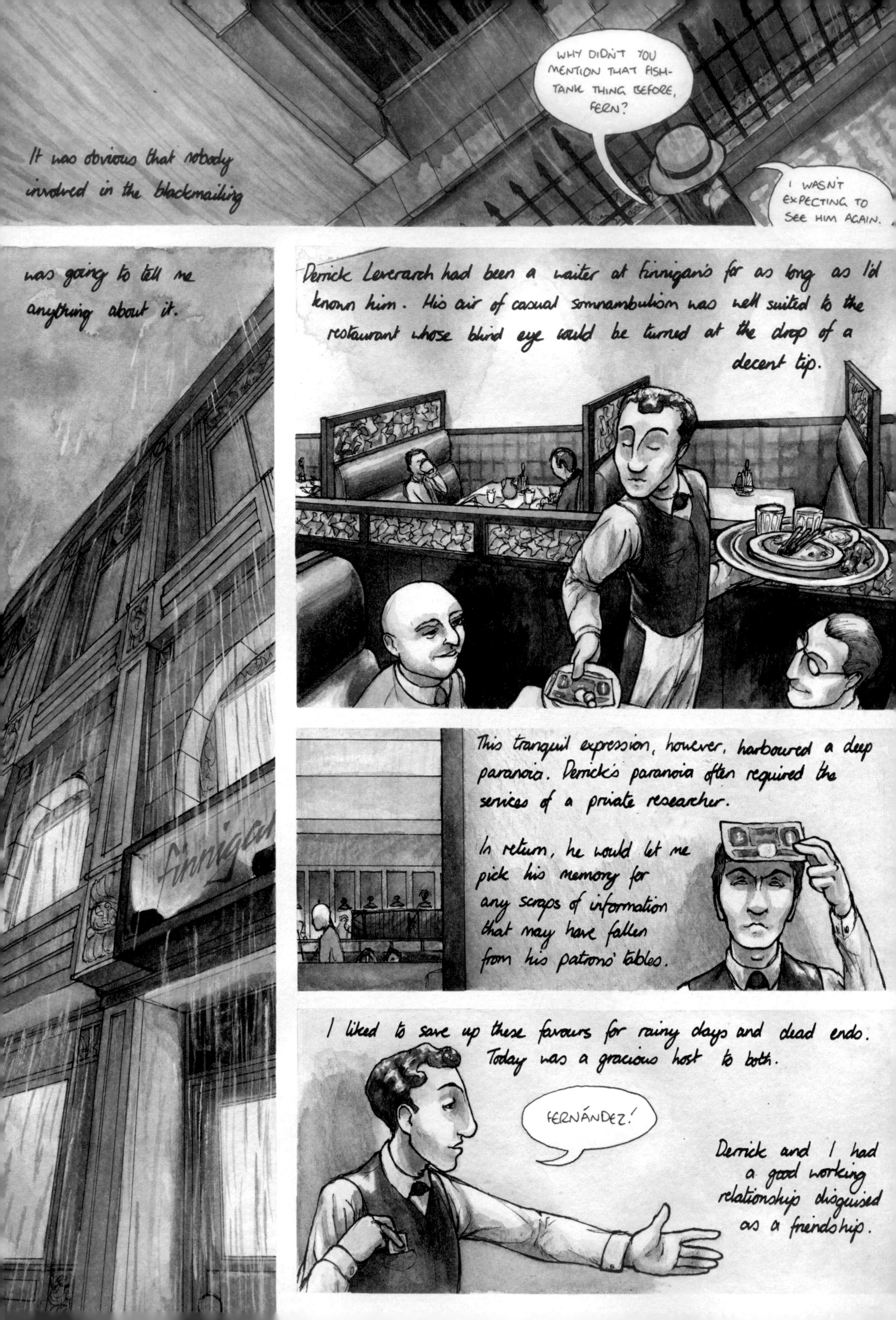

It was obvious that nobody involved in the blackmailing
WHY DIDN'T YOU MENTION THAT FISH-TANK THING BEFORE, FERN?
I WASN'T EXPECTING TO SEE HIM AGAIN.
was going to tell me anything about it.
Derrick Leverarch had been a waiter at Finnigan's for as long as I'd known him. His air of casual somnambulism was well suited to the restaurant whose blind eye could be turned at the drop of a decent tip.
This tranquil expression, however, harboured a deep paranoia. Derrick's paranoia often required the services of a private researcher.
In return, he would let me pick his memory for any scraps of information that may have fallen from his patrons' tables.
I liked to save up these favours for rainy days and dead ends. Today was a gracious host to both.
FERNÁNDEZ!
Derrick and I had a good working relationship disguised as a friendship.

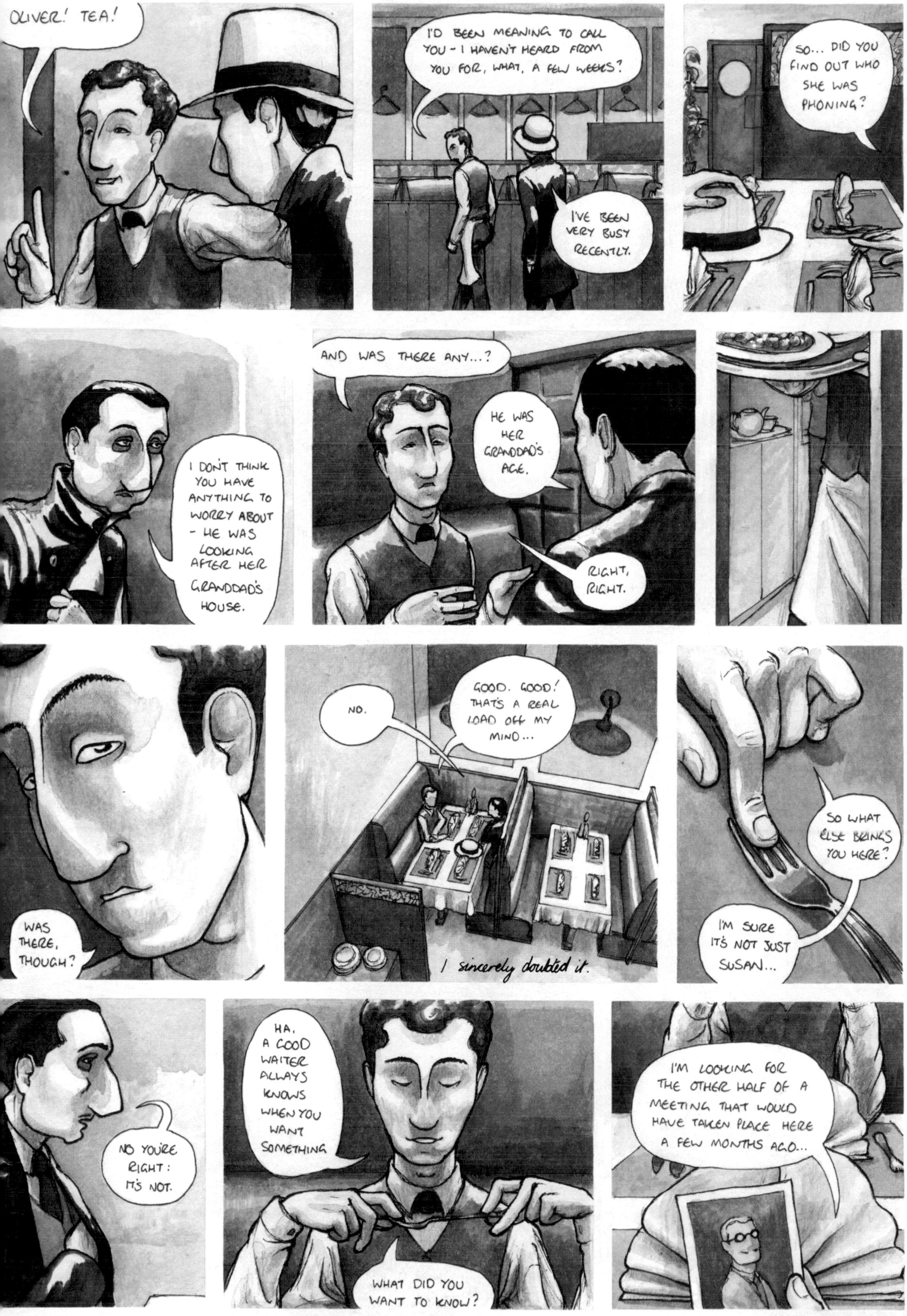
OLIVER! TEA!
I'D BEEN MEANING TO CALL YOU - I HAVEN'T HEARD FROM YOU FOR, WHAT, A FEW WEEKS?
I'VE BEEN VERY BUSY RECENTLY.
SO... DID YOU FIND OUT WHO SHE WAS PHONING?
I DON'T THINK YOU HAVE ANYTHING TO WORRY ABOUT - HE WAS LOOKING AFTER HER GRANDDAD'S HOUSE.
AND WAS THERE ANY...?
HE WAS HER GRANDDAD'S AGE.
RIGHT, RIGHT.
WAS THERE, THOUGH?
NO.
GOOD. GOOD! THAT'S A REAL LOAD OFF MY MIND...
I sincerely doubted it.
SO WHAT ELSE BRINGS YOU HERE?
I'M SURE IT'S NOT JUST SUSAN...
NO YOU'RE RIGHT: IT'S NOT.
HA. A GOOD WAITER ALWAYS KNOWS WHEN YOU WANT SOMETHING
WHAT DID YOU WANT TO KNOW?
I'M LOOKING FOR THE OTHER HALF OF A MEETING THAT WOULD HAVE TAKEN PLACE HERE A FEW MONTHS AGO...

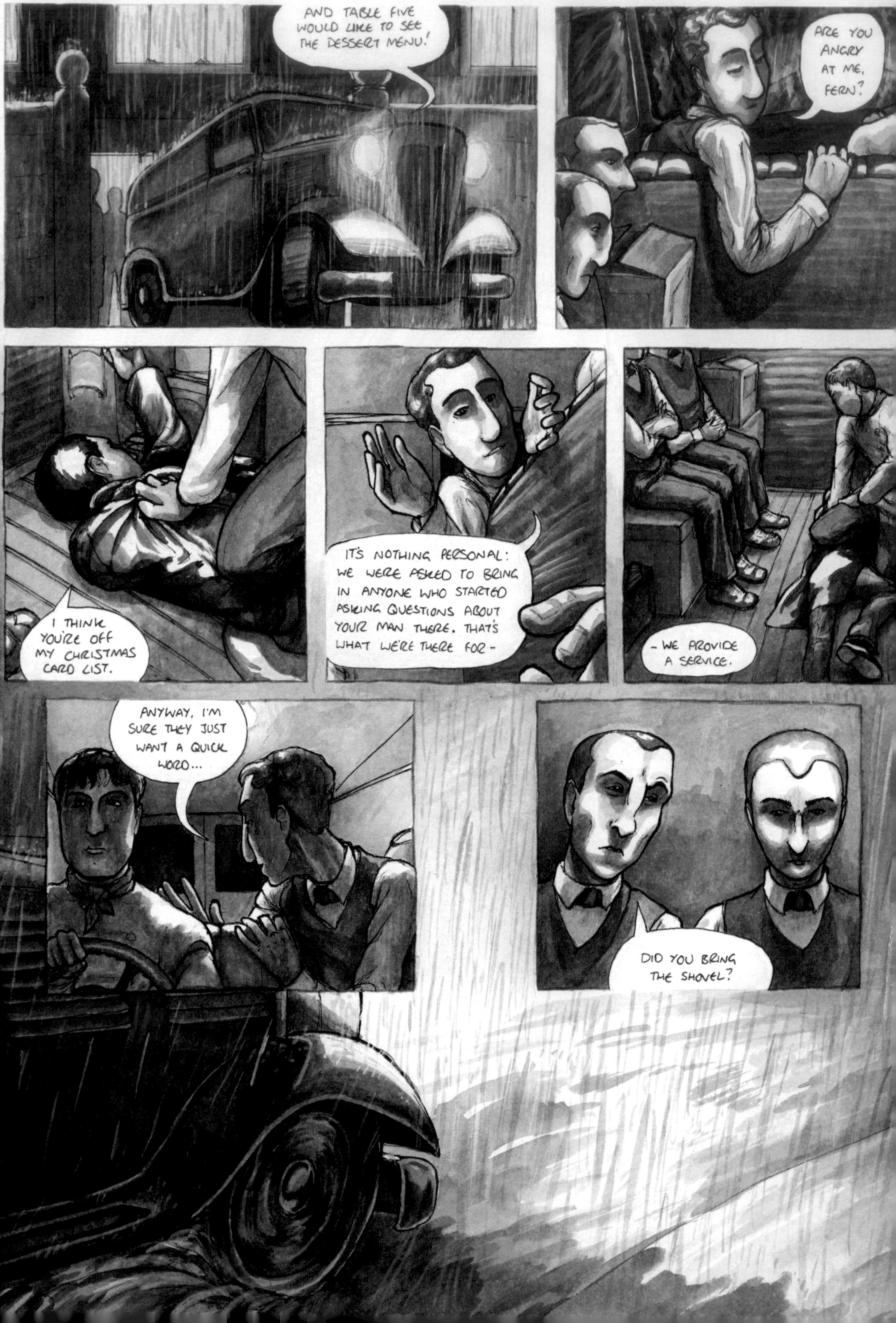
AND TABLE FIVE WOULD LIKE TO SEE THE DESSERT MENU!
ARE YOU ANGRY AT ME, FERN?
I THINK YOU'RE OFF MY CHRISTMAS CARD LIST.
IT'S NOTHING PERSONAL: WE WERE ASKED TO BRING IN ANYONE WHO STARTED ASKING QUESTIONS ABOUT YOUR MAN THERE. THAT'S WHAT WE'RE THERE FOR-
- WE PROVIDE A SERVICE.
ANYWAY, I'M SURE THEY JUST WANT A QUICK WORD...
DID YOU BRING THE SHOVEL?

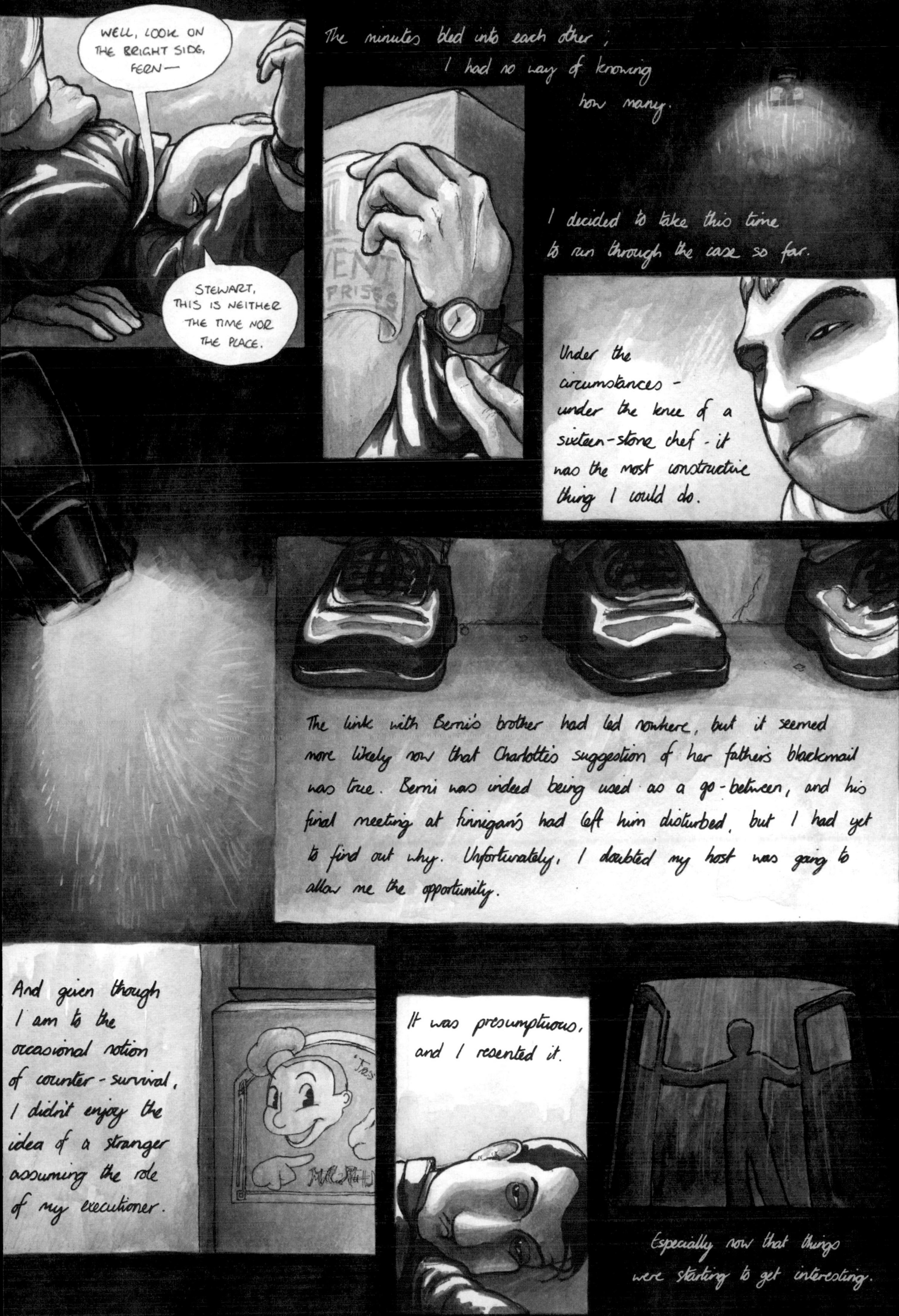

WELL, LOOK ON THE BRIGHT SIDE, FERN—
STEWART, THIS IS NEITHER THE TIME NOR THE PLACE.
The minutes bled into each other; I had no way of knowing how many.
I decided to take this time to run through the case so far.
Under the circumstances - under the knee of a sixteen-stone chef - it was the most constructive thing I could do.
The link with Berni's brother had led nowhere, but it seemed more likely now that Charlotte's suggestion of her father's blackmail was true. Berni was indeed being used as a go-between, and his final meeting at Finnigan's had left him disturbed, but I had yet to find out why. Unfortunately, I doubted my host was going to allow me the opportunity.
And given though I am to the occasional notion of counter-survival, I didn't enjoy the idea of a stranger assuming the role of my executioner.
It was presumptuous, and I resented it.
Especially now that things were starting to get interesting.

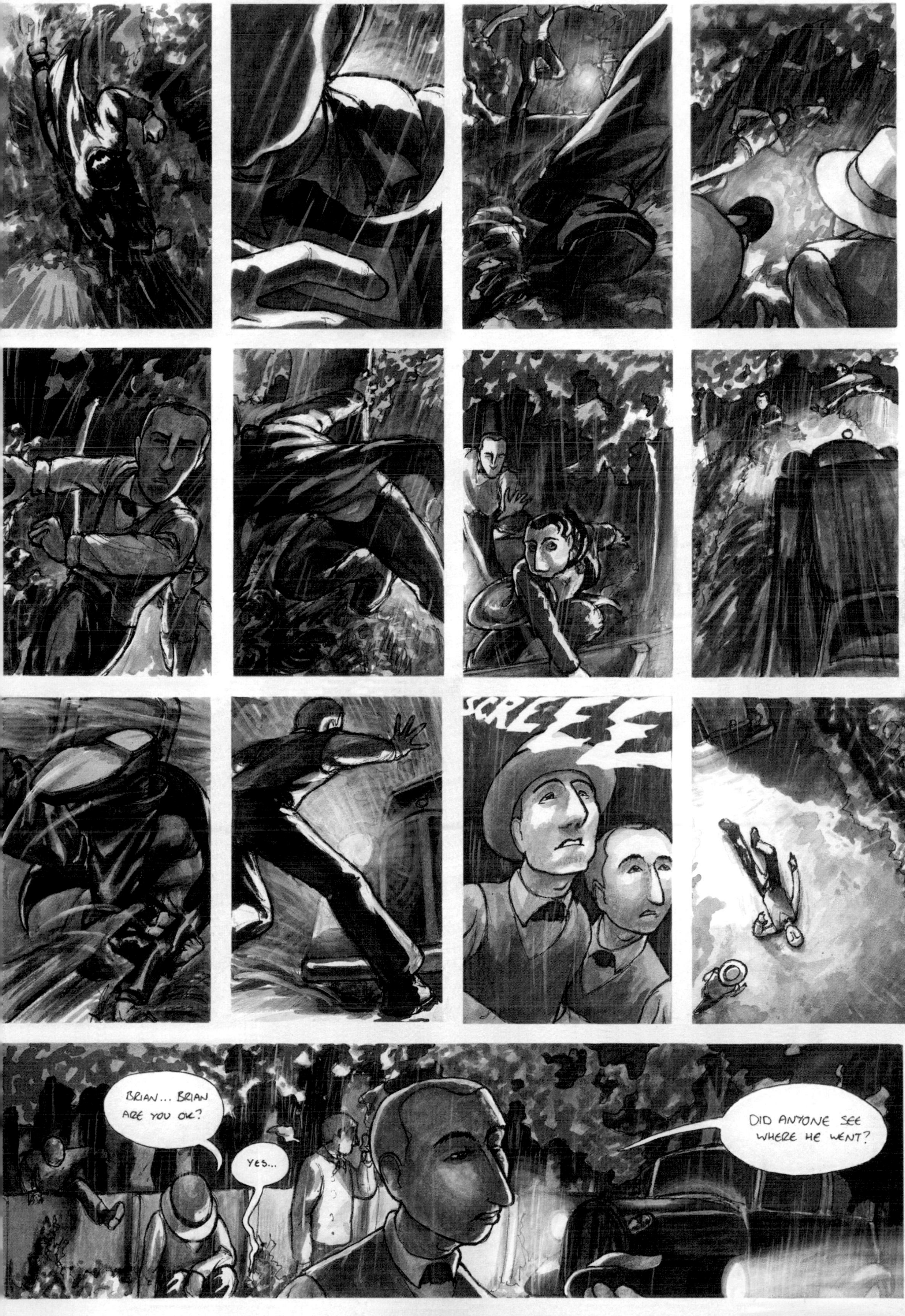
SCREEE
BRIAN... BRIAN ARE YOU OK?
YES...
DID ANYONE SEE WHERE HE WENT?

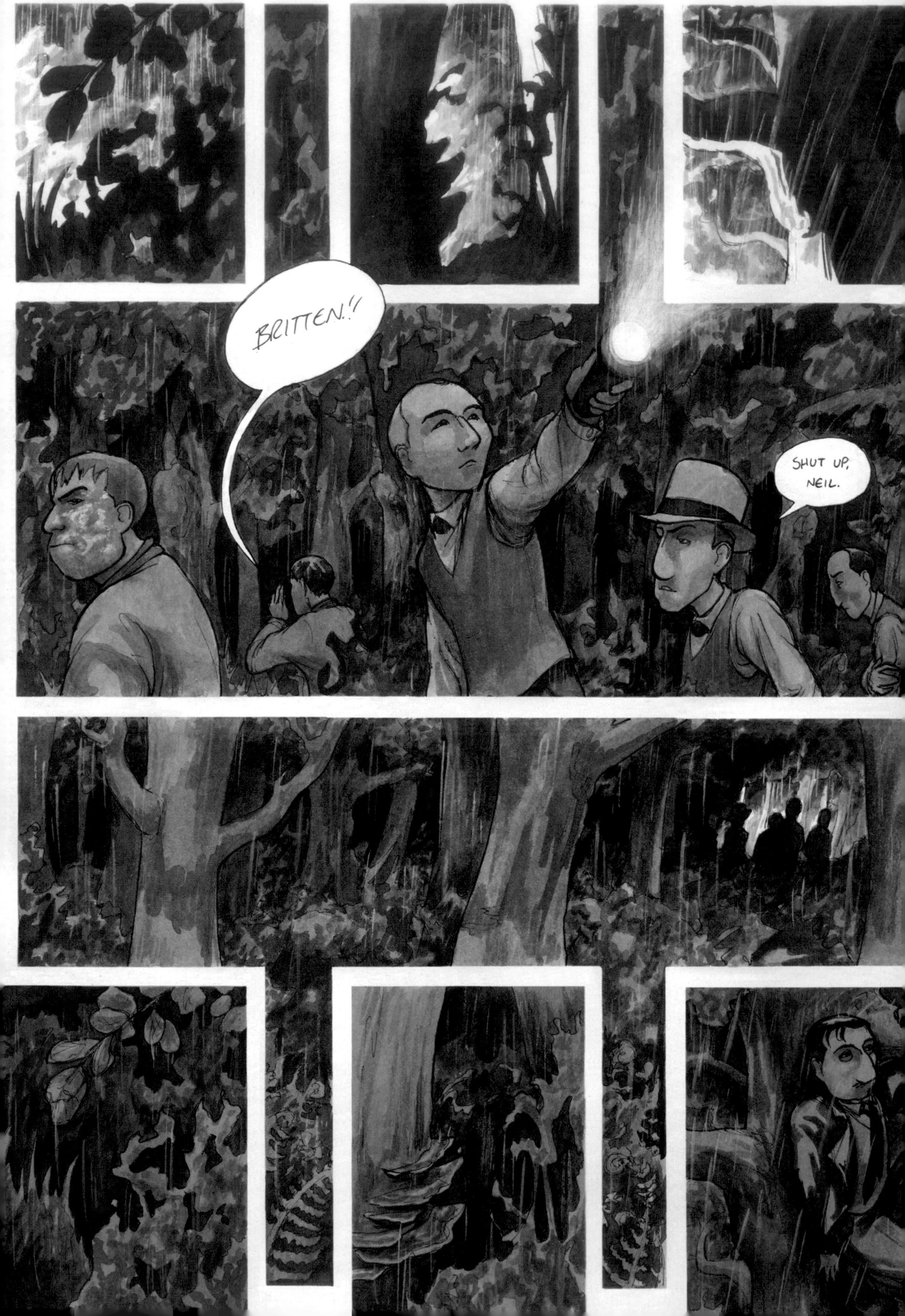
BRITTEN!!
SHUT UP, NEIL.

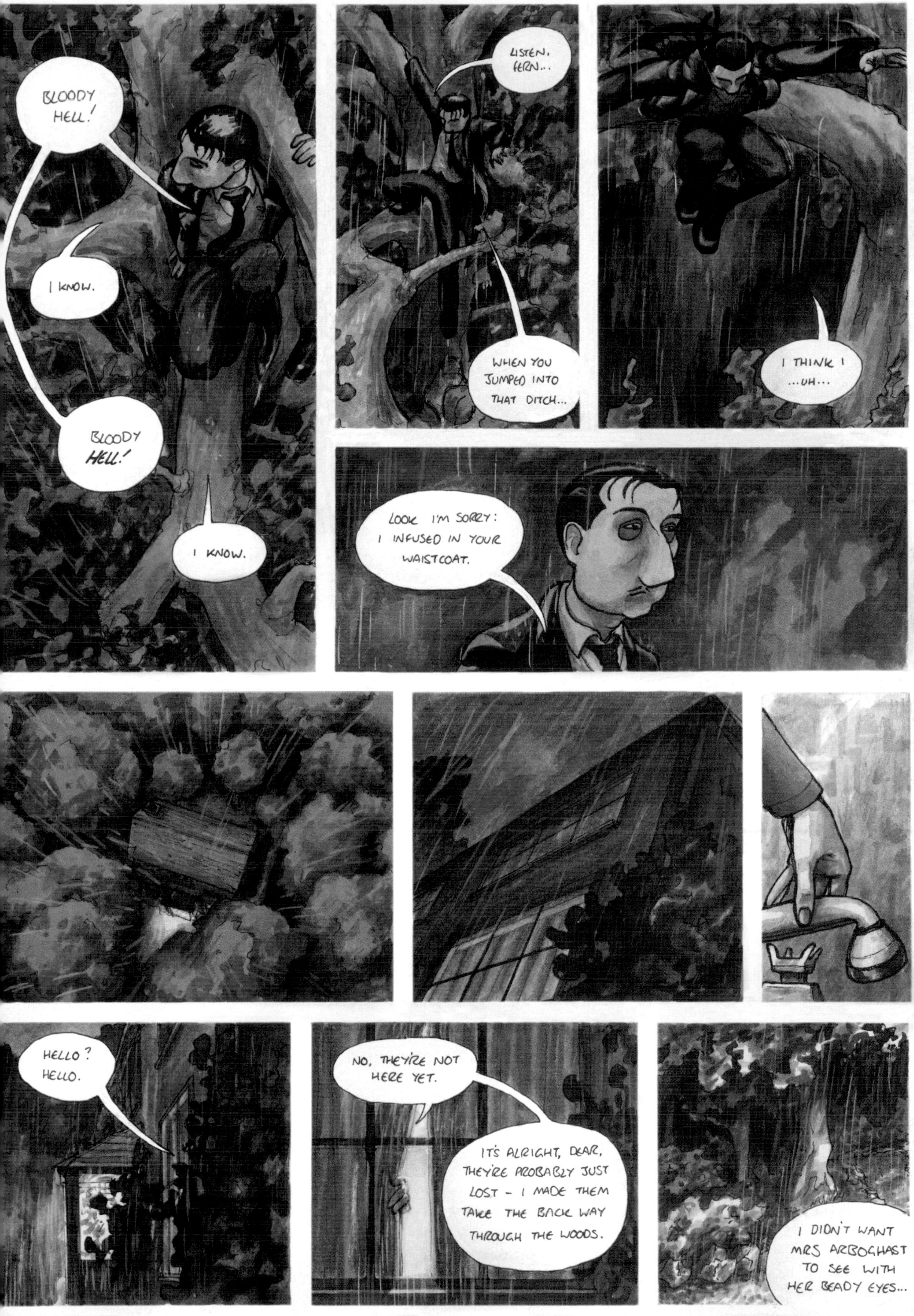

BLOODY HELL!
I KNOW.
BLOODY HELL!
I KNOW.
LISTEN, FERN...
WHEN YOU JUMPED INTO THAT DITCH...
I THINK I ...UH...
LOOK I'M SORRY: I INFUSED IN YOUR WAISTCOAT.
HELLO? HELLO.
NO, THEY'RE NOT HERE YET.
IT'S ALRIGHT, DEAR, THEY'RE PROBABLY JUST LOST - I MADE THEM TAKE THE BACK WAY THROUGH THE WOODS.
I DIDN'T WANT MRS ARBOGHAST TO SEE WITH HER BEADY EYES...

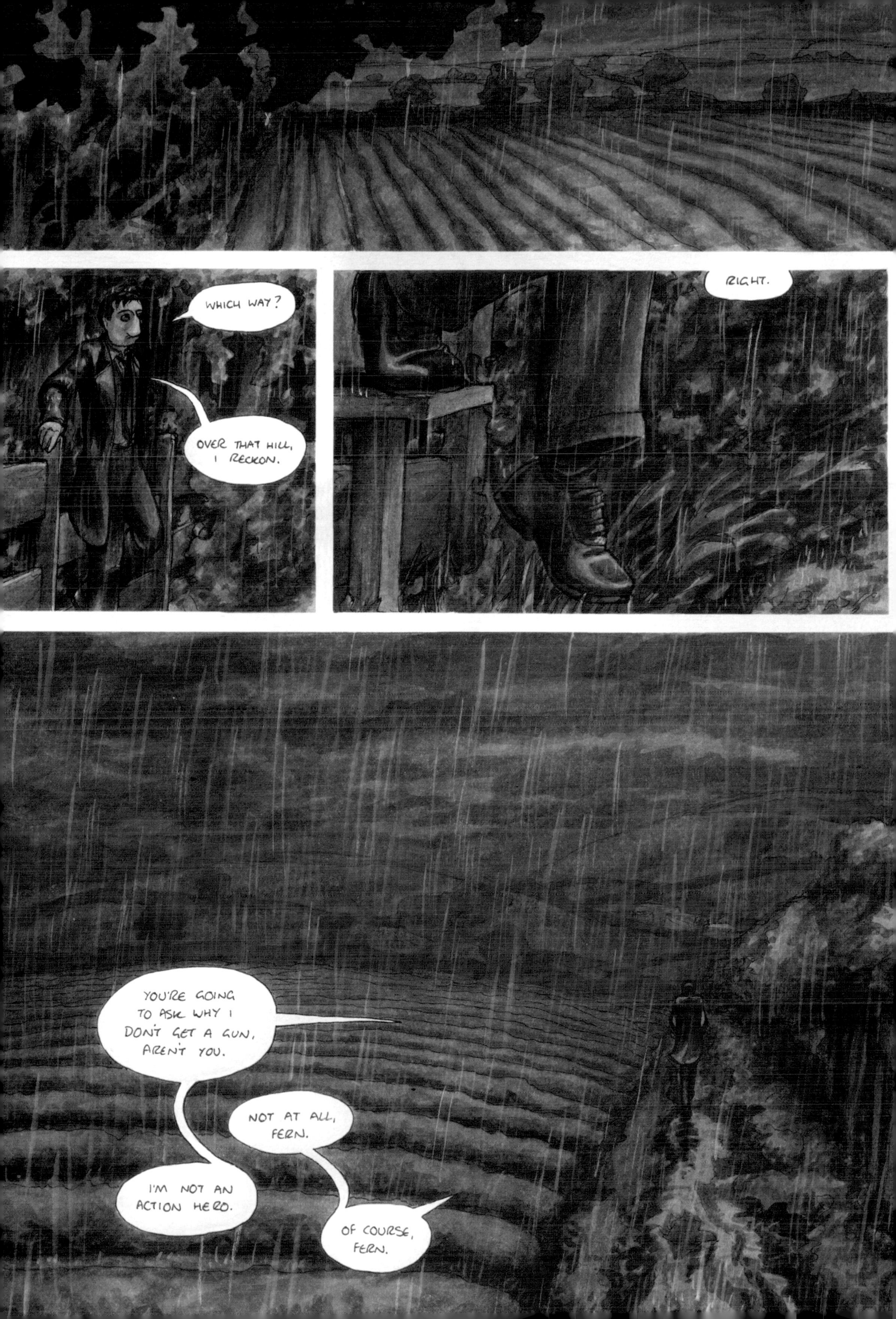
WHICH WAY?
OVER THAT HILL, I RECKON.
RIGHT.
YOU'RE GOING TO ASK WHY I DON'T GET A GUN, AREN'T YOU.
NOT AT ALL, FERN.
I'M NOT AN ACTION HERO.
OF COURSE, FERN.

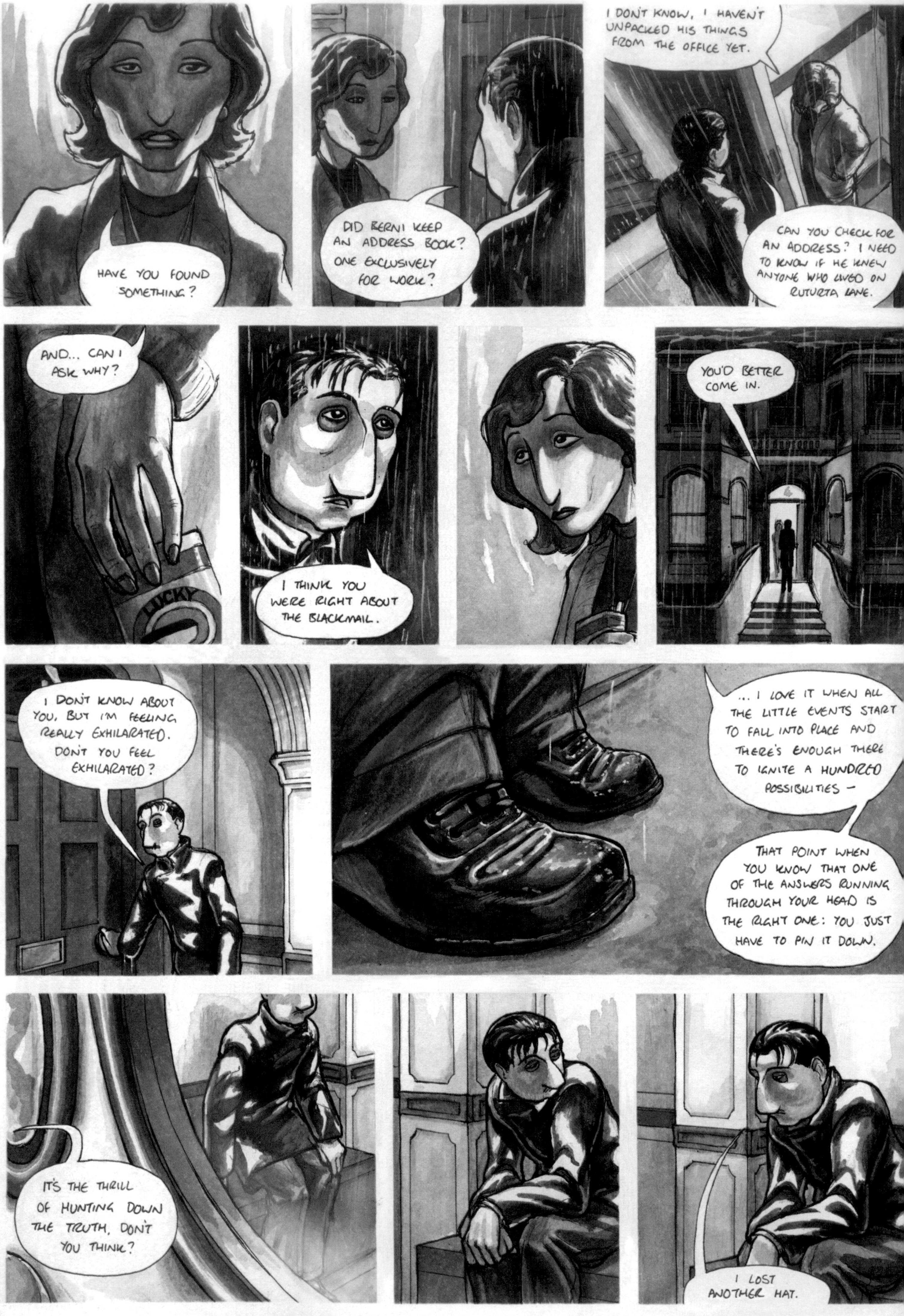
HAVE YOU FOUND SOMETHING?
DID BERNI KEEP AN ADDRESS BOOK? ONE EXCLUSIVELY FOR WORK?
I DON'T KNOW, I HAVEN'T UNPACKED HIS THINGS FROM THE OFFICE YET.
CAN YOU CHECK FOR AN ADDRESS? I NEED TO KNOW IF HE KNEW ANYONE WHO LIVED ON RUTURTA LANE.
AND... CAN I ASK WHY?
LUCKY
I THINK YOU WERE RIGHT ABOUT THE BLACKMAIL.
YOU'D BETTER COME IN.
I DON'T KNOW ABOUT YOU, BUT I'M FEELING REALLY EXHILARATED. DON'T YOU FEEL EXHILARATED?
... I LOVE IT WHEN ALL THE LITTLE EVENTS START TO FALL INTO PLACE AND THERE'S ENOUGH THERE TO IGNITE A HUNDRED POSSIBILITIES –
THAT POINT WHEN YOU KNOW THAT ONE OF THE ANSWERS RUNNING THROUGH YOUR HEAD IS THE RIGHT ONE: YOU JUST HAVE TO PIN IT DOWN.
IT'S THE THRILL OF HUNTING DOWN THE TRUTH, DON'T YOU THINK?
I LOST ANOTHER HAT.

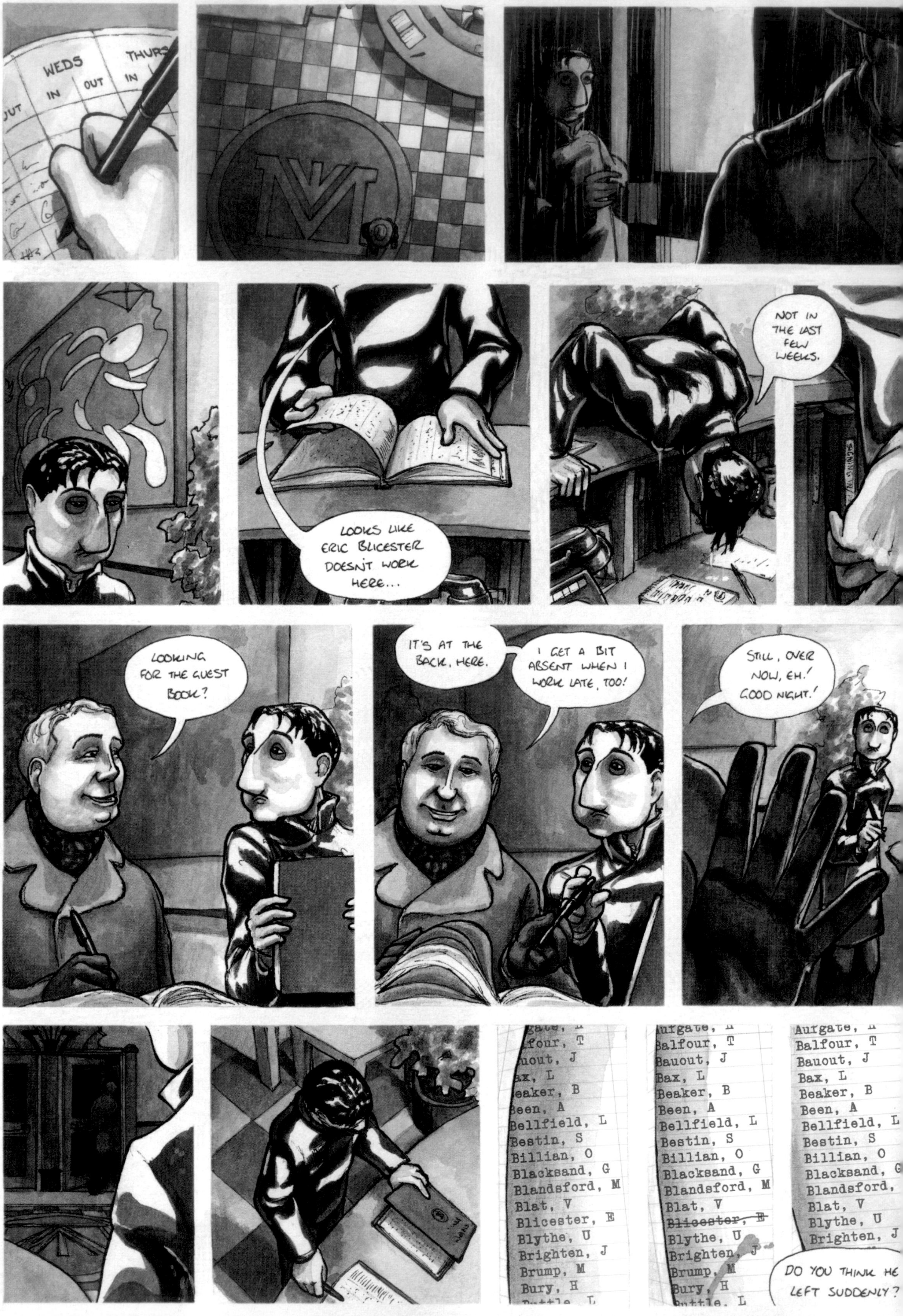
WEDS
THURS
IN
OUT
IN
LOOKS LIKE ERIC BLICESTER DOESN'T WORK HERE...
NOT IN THE LAST FEW WEEKS.
LOOKING FOR THE GUEST BOOK?
IT'S AT THE BACK, HERE.
I GET A BIT ABSENT WHEN I WORK LATE, TOO!
STILL, OVER NOW, EH! GOOD NIGHT!
Beaker, B
Been, A
Bellfield, L
Bestin, S
Billian, O
Blacksand, G
Blandsford, M
Blat, V
Blicester, E
Blythe, U
Brighten, J
Brump, M
Bury, H
Balfour, T
Bax, L
Beaker, B
Been, A
Bellfield, L
Bestin, S
Billian, O
Blacksand, G
Blandsford, M
Blat, V
Blicester, E
Blythe, U
Brump, M
Bury, H
Aurgate, H
Balfour, T
Bauout, J
Bax, L
Beaker, B
Been, A
Bellfield, L
Bestin, S
Billian, O
Blacksand, G
Blat, V
Blythe, U
Brighten, J
DO YOU THINK HE LEFT SUDDENLY?

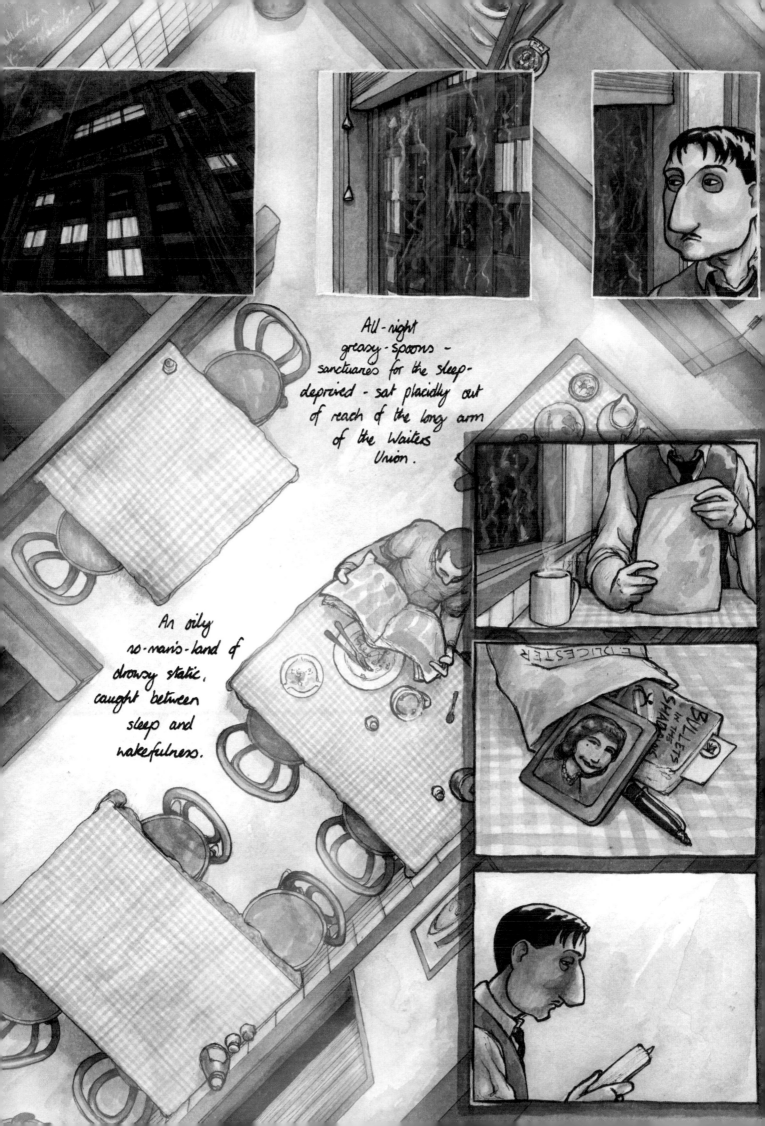

All-night
greasy-spoons -
sanctuaries for the sleep-
deprived - sat placidly out
of reach of the long arm
of the Waiters
Union.

An oily
no-man's-land of
drowsy static,
caught between
sleep and
wakefulness.

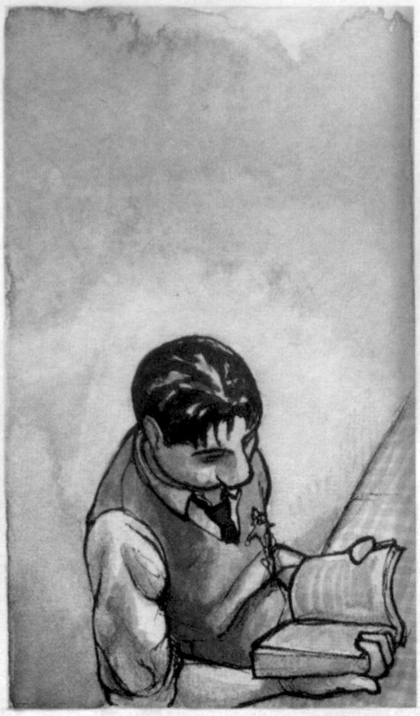

"Blast it, Hamish! Don't you think of anyone but yourself?!"

She stood there, her head cocked like my .45 Colt, and I realised we were playing Russian roulette with the conversation. It was my turn, and I don't like playing games with women. Lack of logic makes them dangerous.

"I think of Janet."

"Janet?" Her laugh refreezes the ice in my drink. "What do you care for Janet?"

"I care enough to see her steer clear of Eisenburgh and his cronies. So if you're after an apology, you'd better take a ticket and join the queue."

Her dainty left hand turns to iron and slaps me hard in the face. I was surprised, but not enough to drop my glass. It was a good scotch. The bracelets on her wrists jangle as she bristles with rage.

"You're a cold, cruel, good-for-nothing bum. Mallery should have left you breathing Pacific while he had the chance!"

"Easy, Dolores, I still got a heart."

She curls her lip like a theatre curtain and treats me to the front row of her snarl.

"If you had a heart I'd see it there on your sleeve next to your cheap cufflinks."

She grinds my doormat under her heel as she storms out of my office, leaving in her wake the scent of rose petals and malice. If this were another time and another place, she'd be alright.

Hell, maybe I'd even love her.

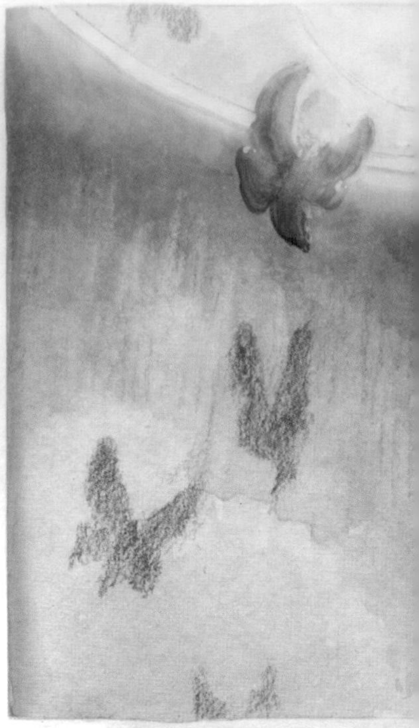

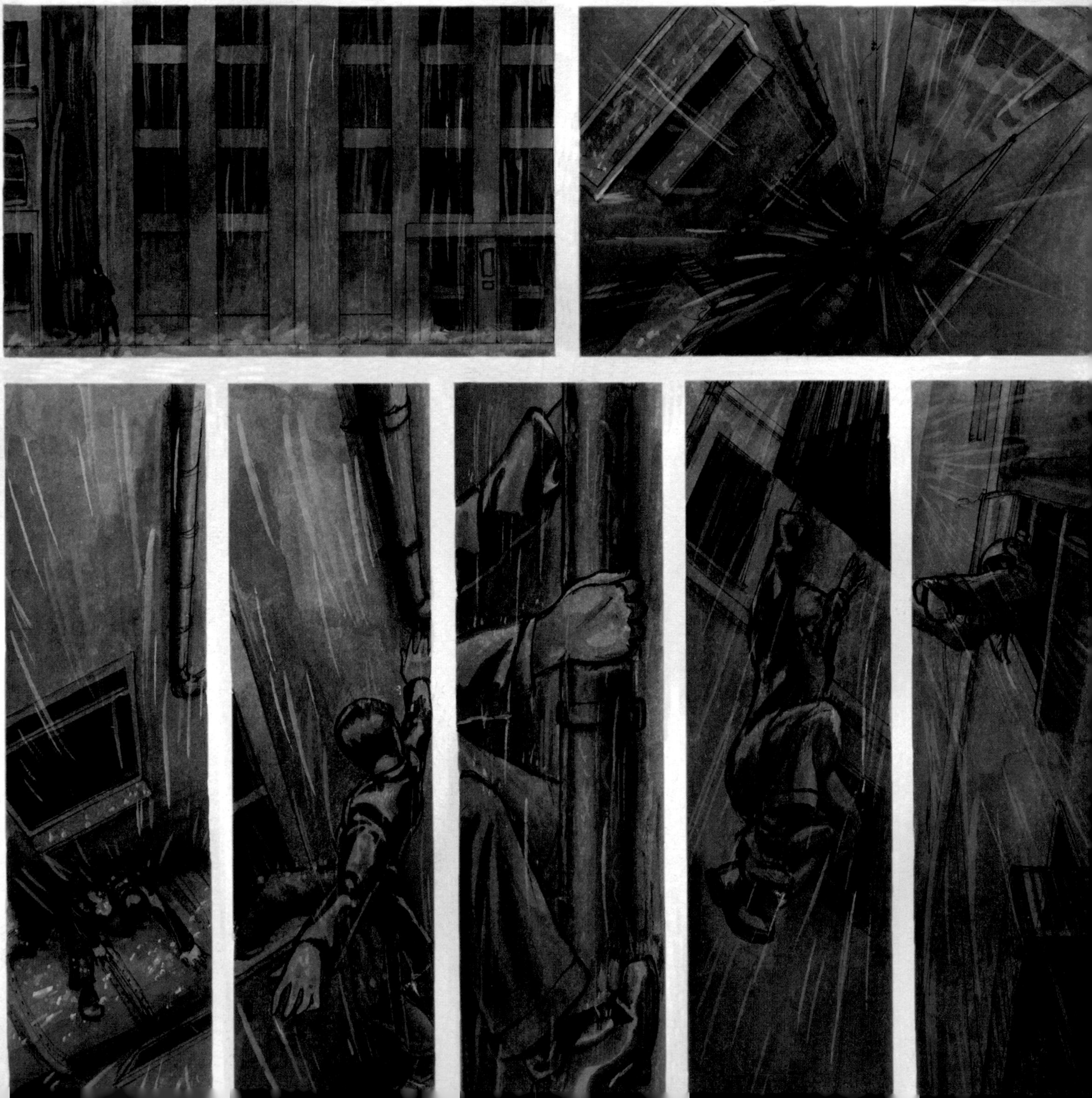

Some careful and discreet questions in some careful and discreet establishments eventually led to Maughton Publishing's other lines of publication.

Lines that wouldn't sit well with their usual readership.

Lines that were neither careful, nor discreet.

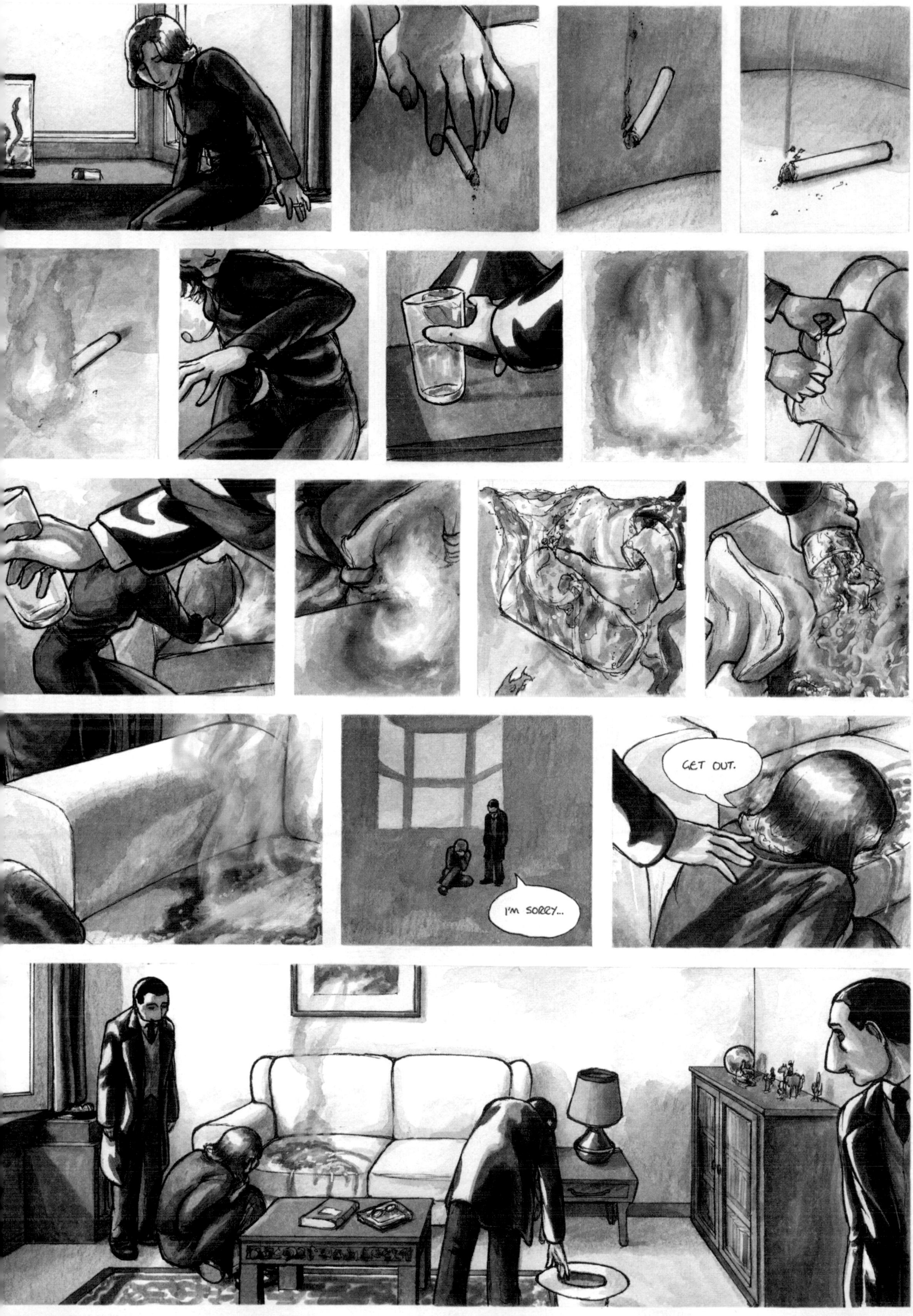
I'M SORRY...
GET OUT.

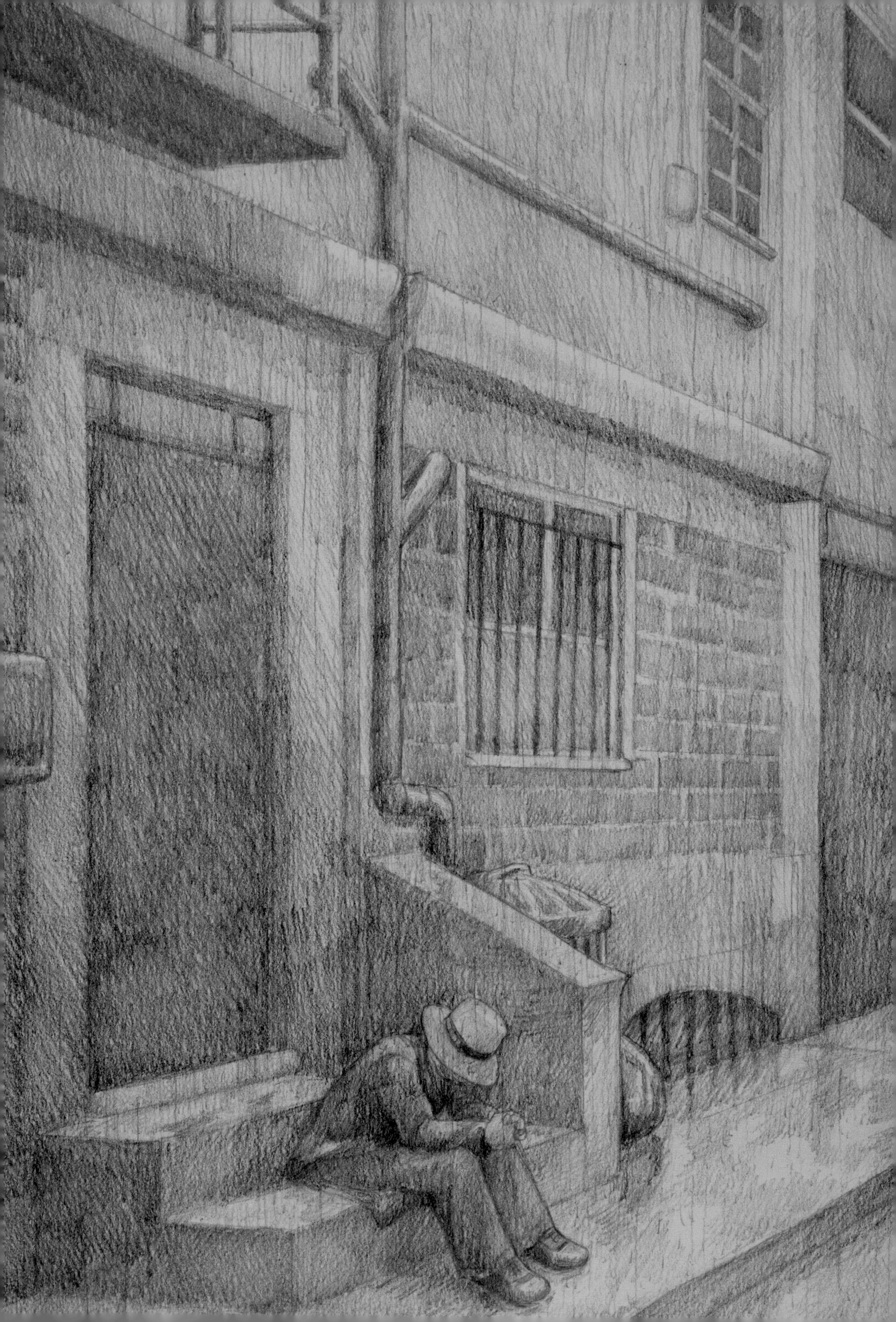

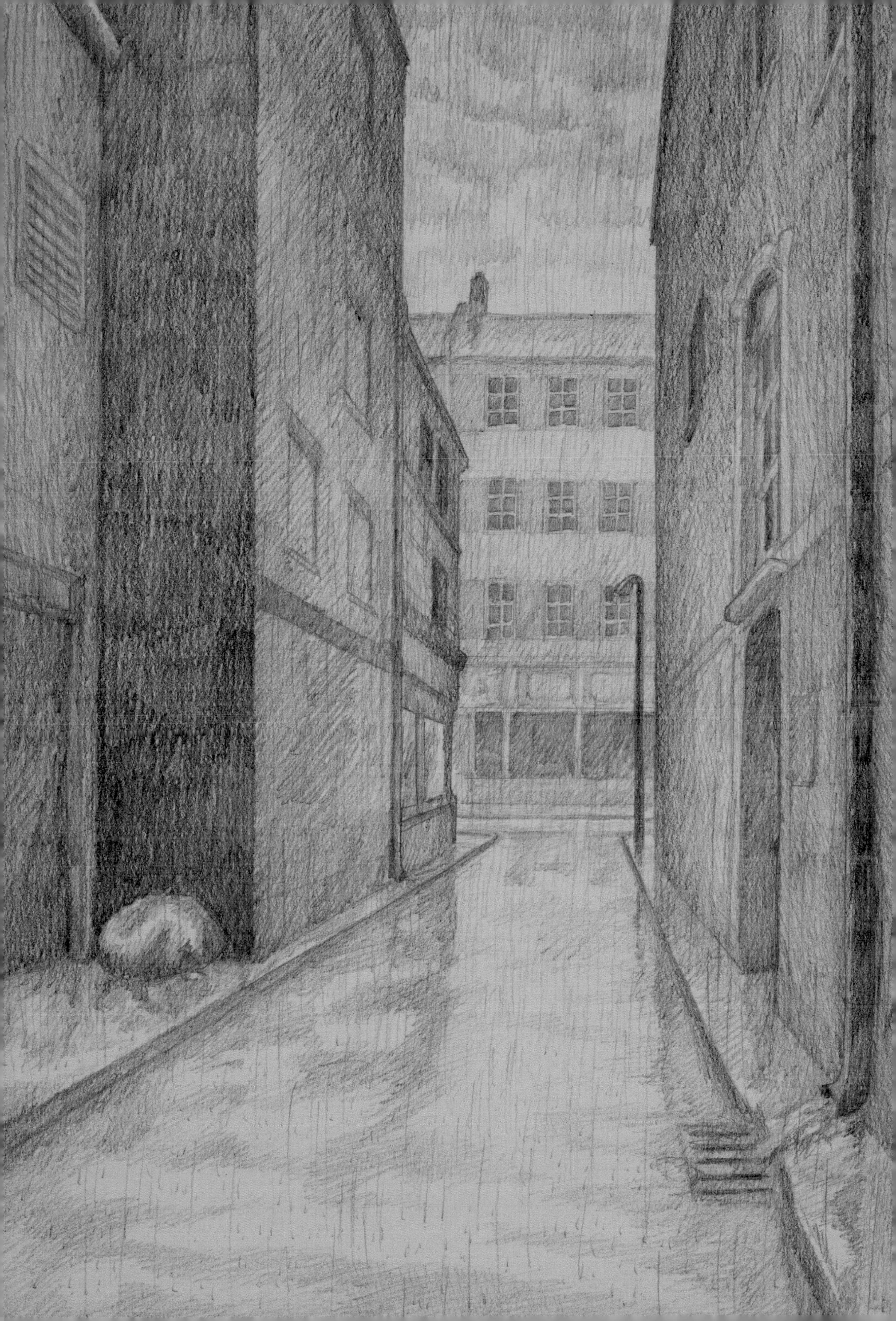

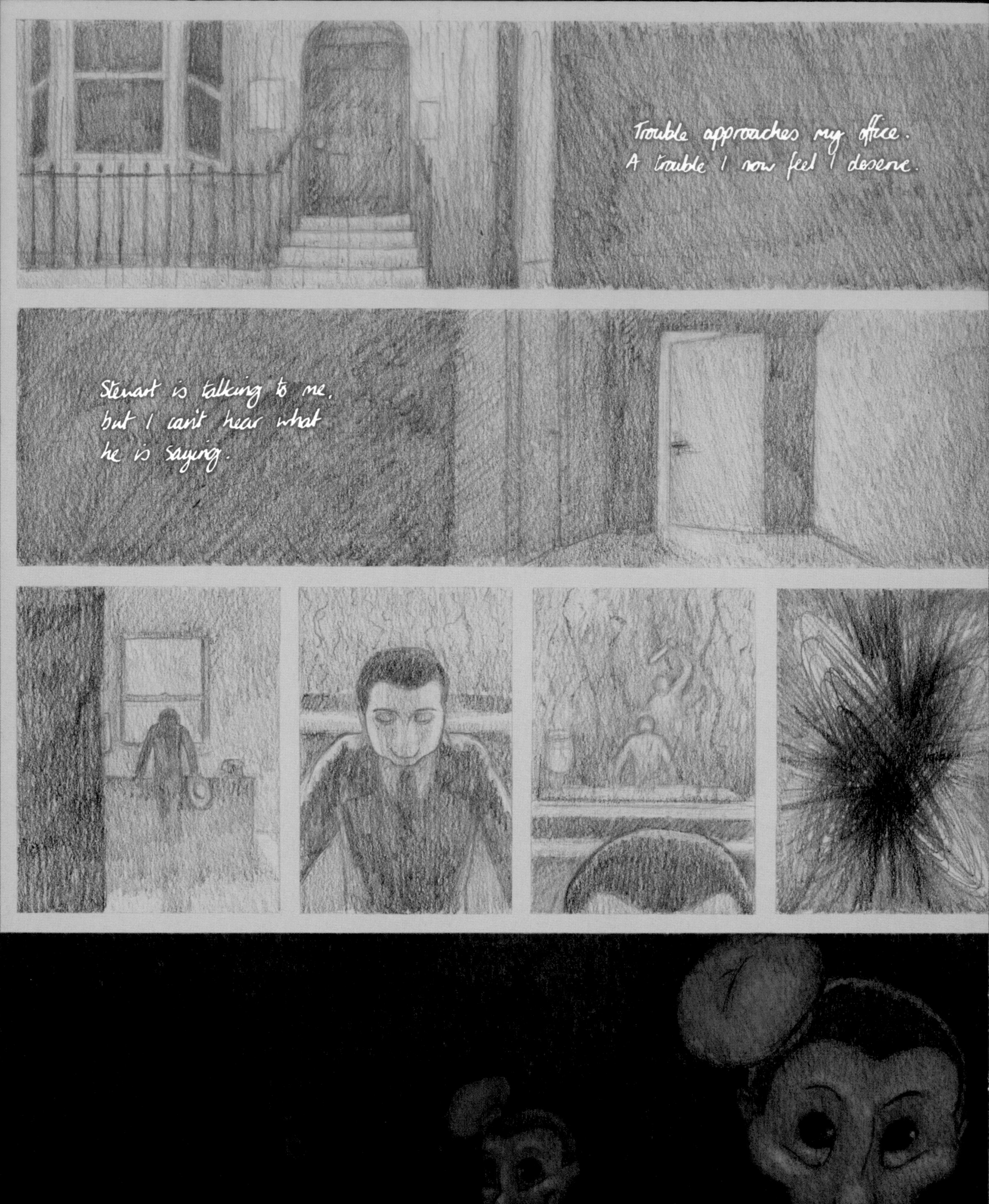
Trouble approaches my office.
A trouble I now feel I deserve.
Stewart is talking to me, but I can't hear what he is saying.

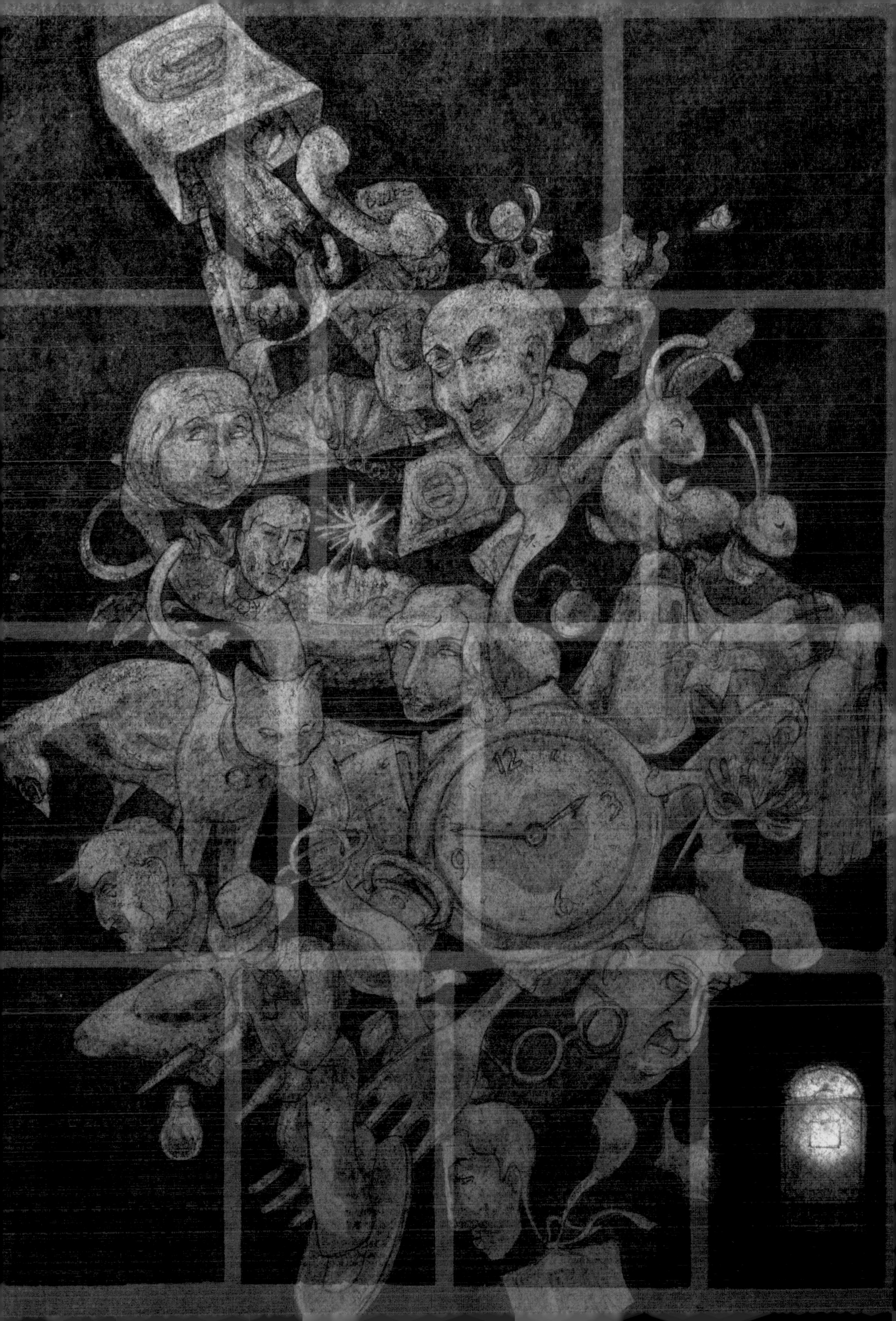

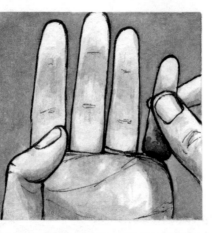

Drugged and nauseous, I was discharged.

The lingering ache a dull requiem for my chances of ever becoming a concert pianist.

I didn't know who had taken it upon themselves to mutilate me, but I suspected the recently bereaved Eric Blicester.

He needn't have worried about my further involvement, though:

His act was a bloody punctuation mark at the end of a regrettable career.

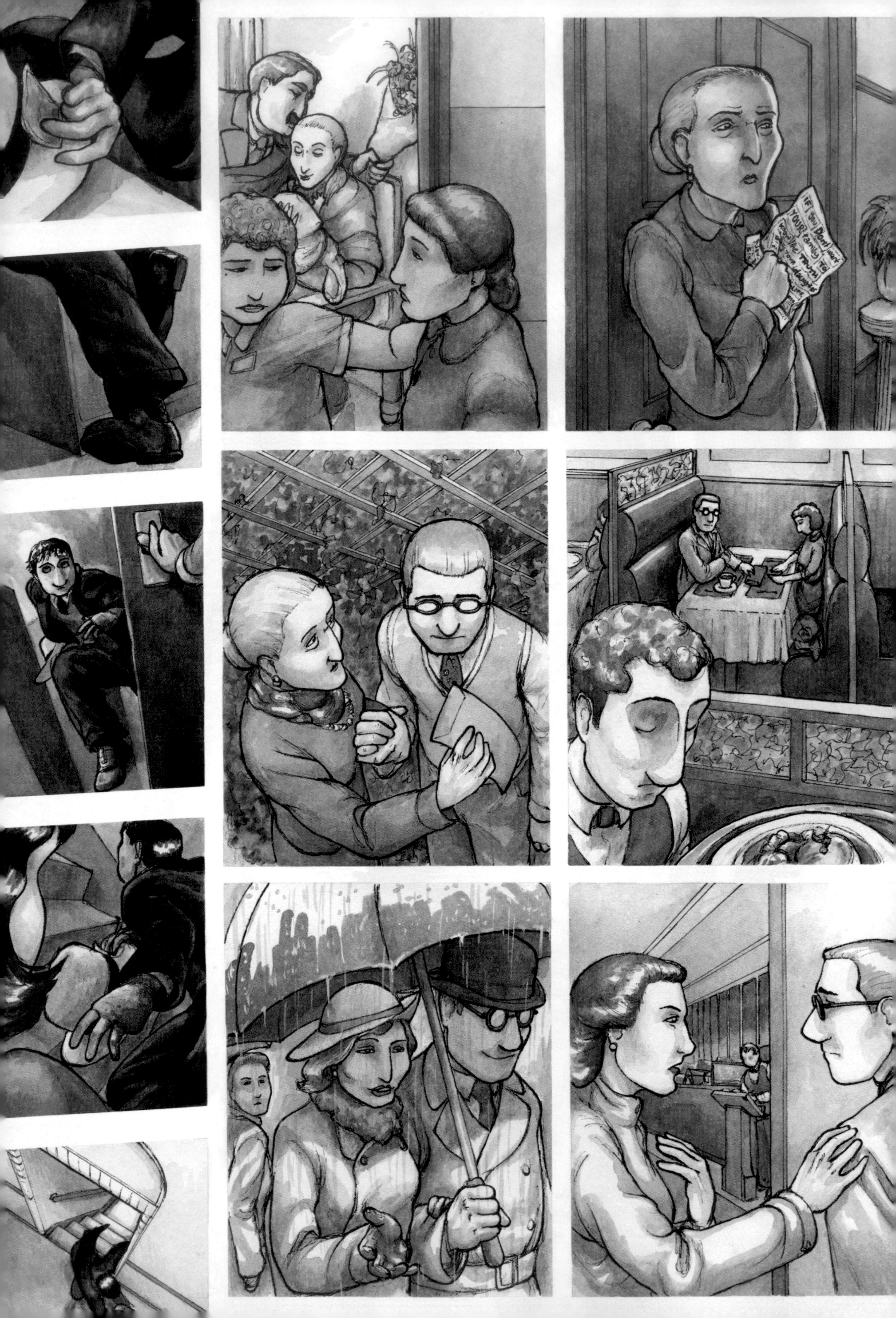
IF you Don't want
YOUR family TO
know the TRUTH
your daughter

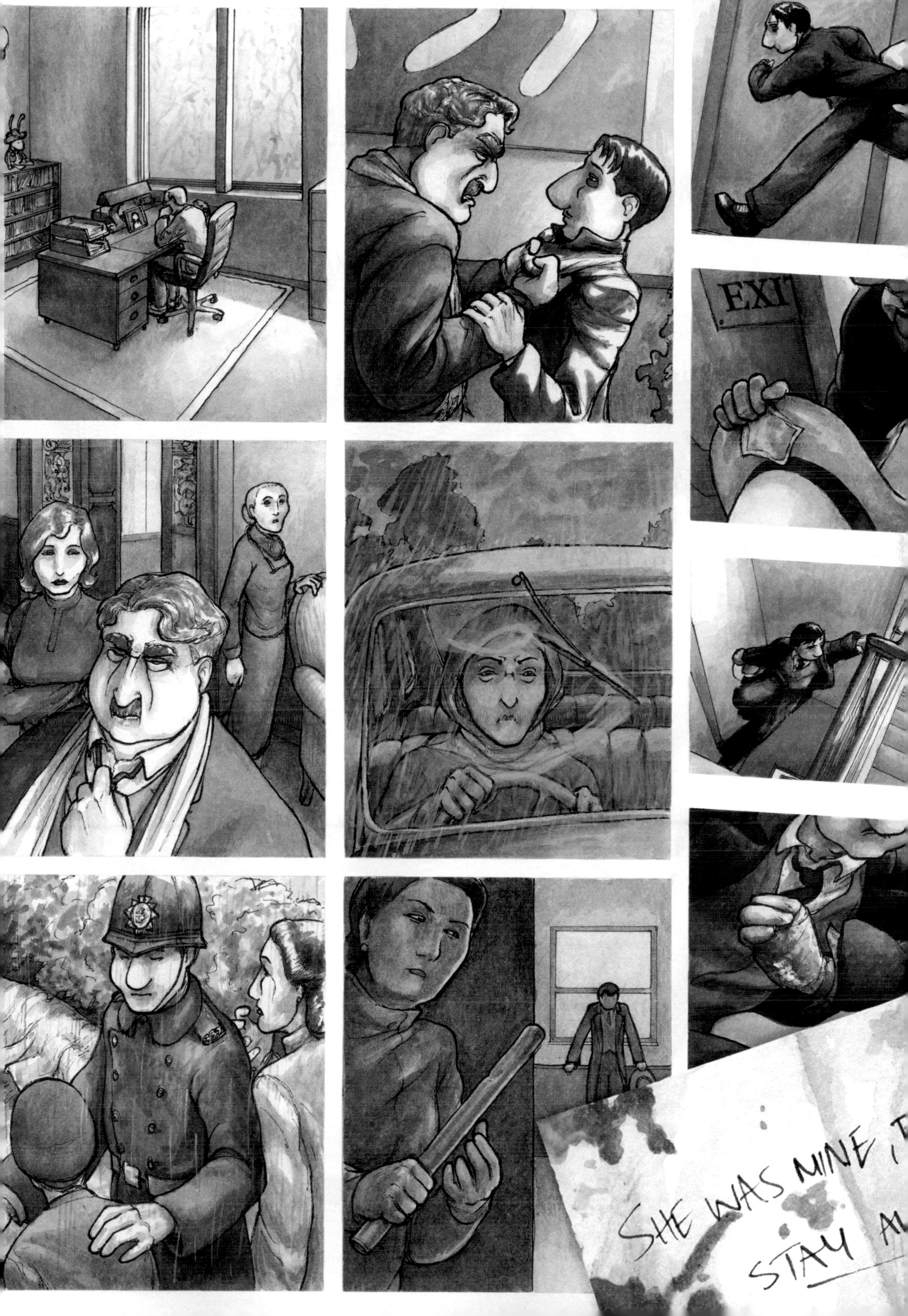
EXIT
SHE WAS MINE
STAY

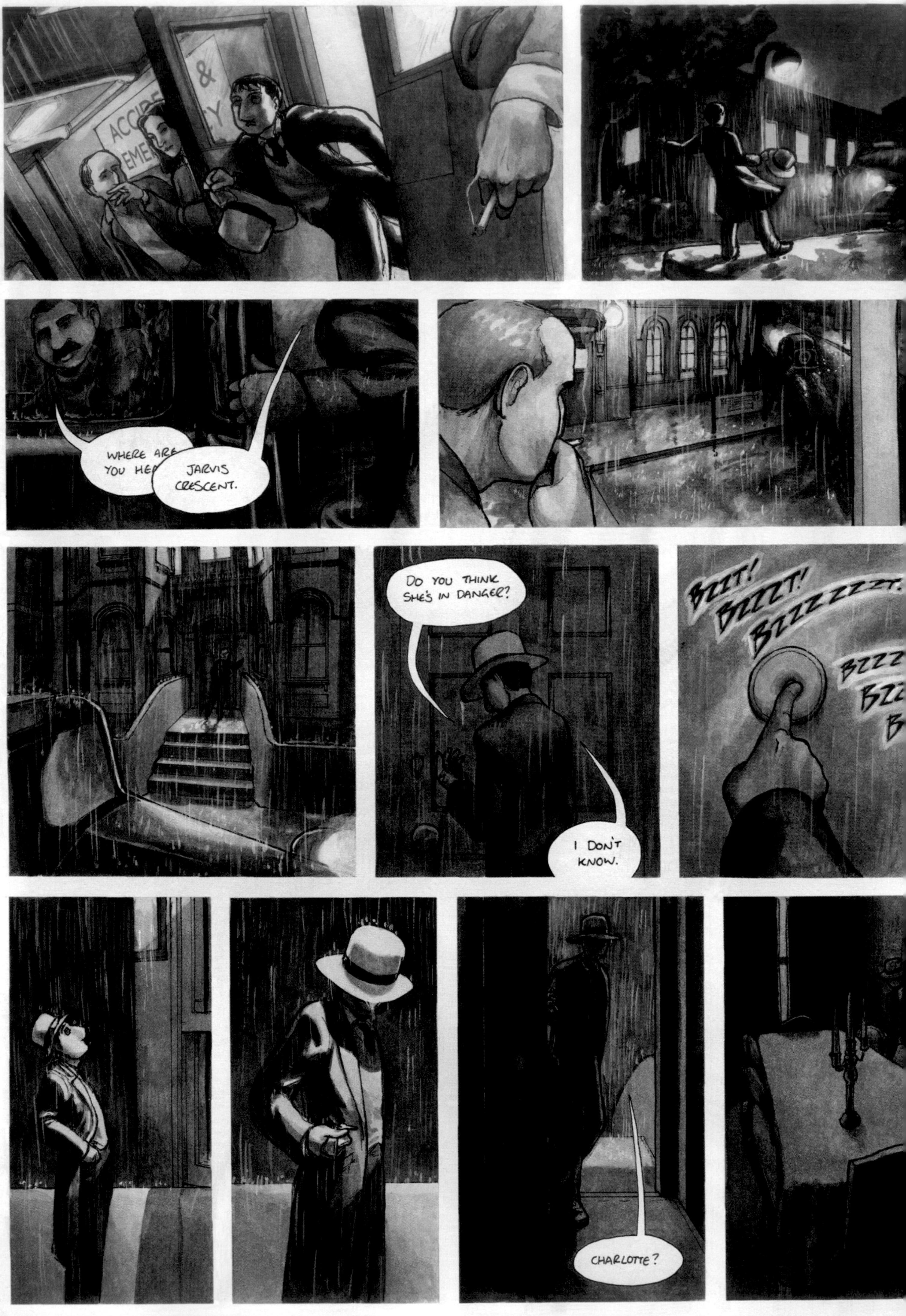

WHERE ARE YOU HEA
JARVIS CRESCENT.
DO YOU THINK SHE'S IN DANGER?
I DON'T KNOW.
BZZT! BZZZT! BZZZZZZZT!
CHARLOTTE?

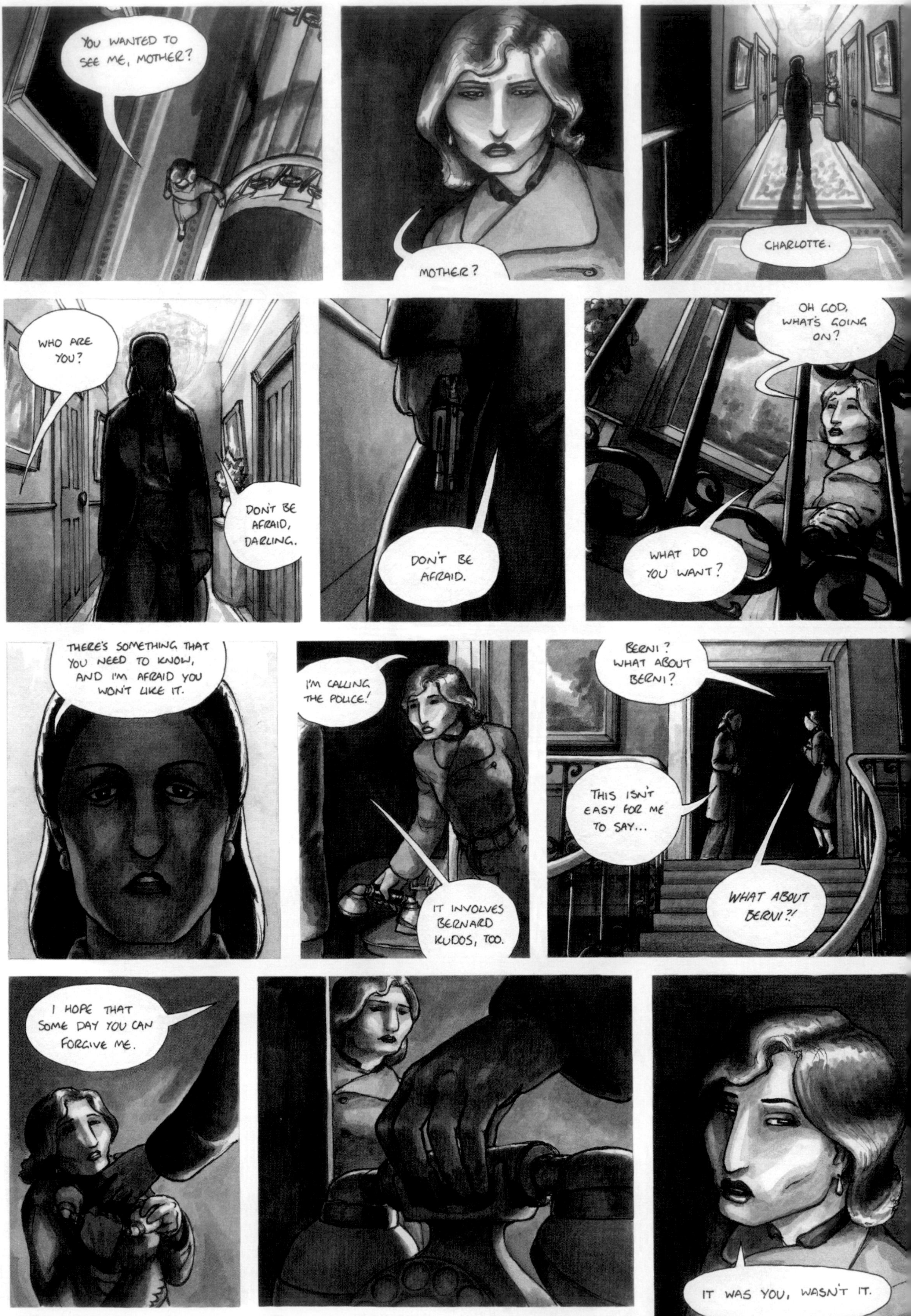
YOU WANTED TO SEE ME, MOTHER?
MOTHER?
CHARLOTTE.
WHO ARE YOU?
DON'T BE AFRAID, DARLING.
DON'T BE AFRAID.
OH GOD, WHAT'S GOING ON?
WHAT DO YOU WANT?
THERE'S SOMETHING THAT YOU NEED TO KNOW, AND I'M AFRAID YOU WON'T LIKE IT.
I'M CALLING THE POLICE!
IT INVOLVES BERNARD KUDOS, TOO.
BERNI? WHAT ABOUT BERNI?
THIS ISN'T EASY FOR ME TO SAY...
WHAT ABOUT BERNI?!
I HOPE THAT SOME DAY YOU CAN FORGIVE ME.
IT WAS YOU, WASN'T IT.

I knew that there were casualties, of course. I knew that Ginny should have been held accountable for Minnie's death. I knew that Eric deserved to know what had happened to his wife, and that Lenora – poor Lenora – as an innocent bystander should never have had this much suffering thrust upon her.

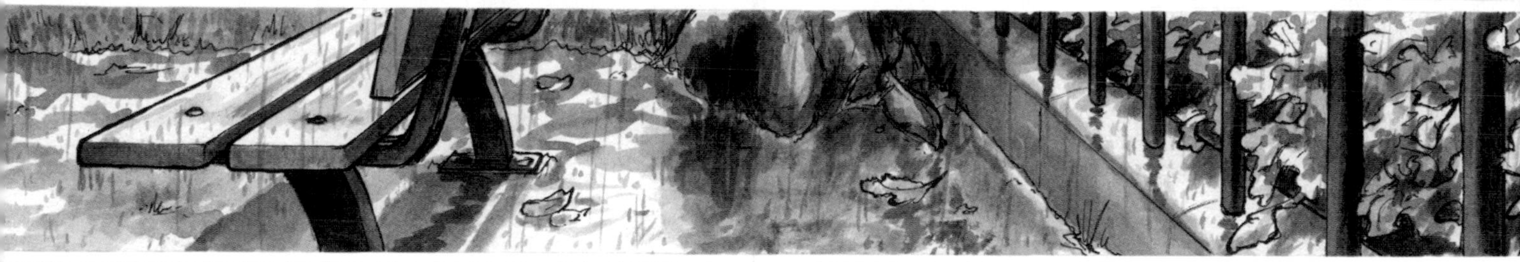

I knew this, yet I did nothing to set the record straight. Perched precariously on top of this ugly hill of lies and deceit was Charlotte's oblivious peace of mind. She was my client, she came to me for help, and I had a responsibility to her. Absolute morality is a luxury for the short-sighted.

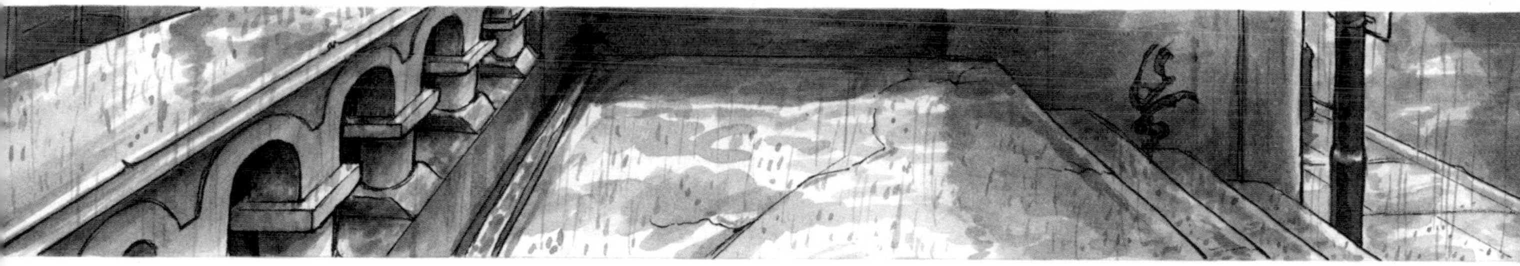

By the time the police had arrived, Frances was long dead – her neck broken during the fall. The Maughtons evidently had powerful friends, as no investigation ever took place.

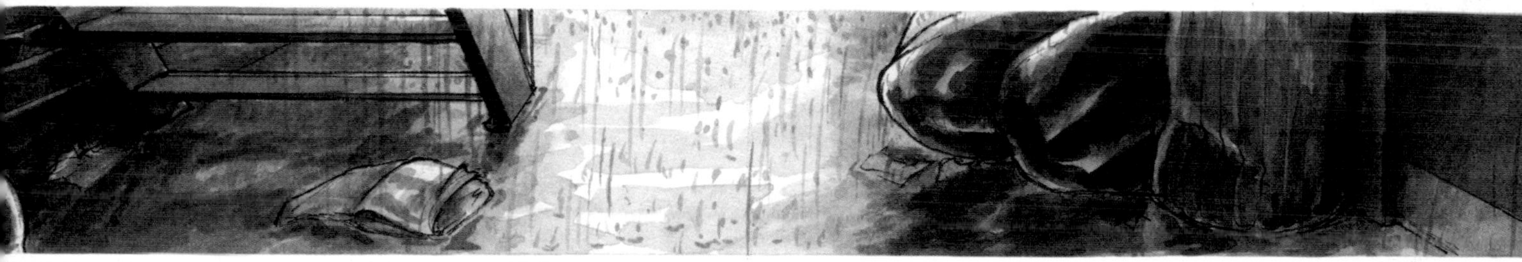

Charlotte concluded, when told about Michael Kudos leaving Frances alone to bear his illegitimate child, that Frances must have killed Berni out of cold-blooded revenge. I didn't redirect her: she was partly right in her conclusion.

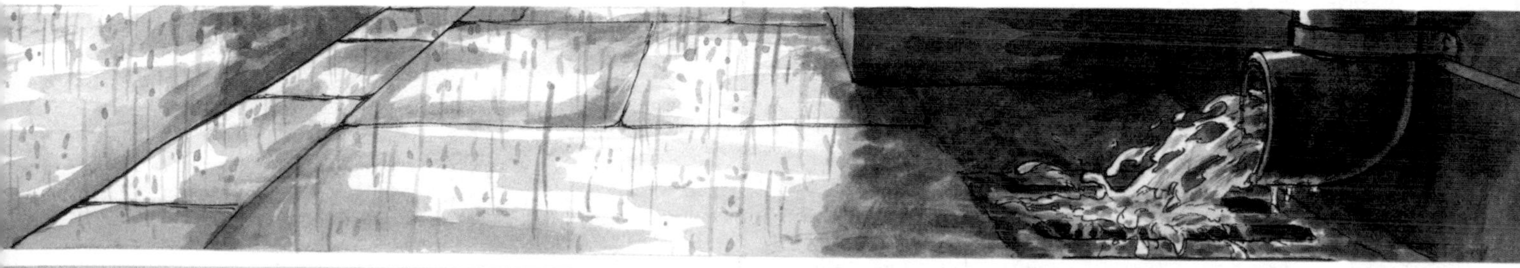

In telling him that his fiancée was his own brother's daughter, Frances left Berni trapped with an incredible, undeniable truth. Forced to choose between his incestuous marriage and a revelation that would destroy both the family that had accepted him so readily and the girl he was devoted to, he took his own life.

After I left the Maughtons' house for the last time, I went
  to my office and destroyed the file, burning it to ashes.
Once I'd started, there seemed no reason to stop. My other cases;
my life's work; files and files and every one a compilation of
wretched misery, a window onto infinite sadness...
      I burned them all.

  I have wielded the truth for sixteen long years, the name
  'Heartbreaker' perched on my shoulder like a vulture. The grand
    finale I nairely waited for never came, and the absolution
    I was so desperate to find has eluded me to the end.

But at least I have saved one person
              from the truth.

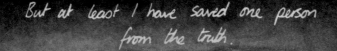